family circle®

homemade Jams & Preserves

CONFIDENT COOKING

The Family Circle® Promise of Success

Welcome to the world of Confident Cooking,
created for you in the Australian **Family Circle®
Test Kitchen,** where recipes are double-tested by
our team of home economists to achieve a
high standard of success—and delicious
results every time.

M U R D O C H   B O O K S®

Sydney • London • Vancouver • New York

C O N T E

Peach Conserve, page 21

Grape Jelly, page 38

Pineapple and Mango Jam, page 37

Traditional Fruit Mince, page 34

N T S

Melon and Lemon Conserve, page 43

Chilli and Red Capsicum Relish, page 68

The Publisher thanks the following for their assistance: Chief Australia, Sunbeam Corporation Ltd, Kambrook, Sheldon & Hammond, Bertoli Olive Oil; Southcorp Appliances; Queensland Fruit & Vegetable Growers.
Front cover: Quince Jelly (page 26).
Inside front cover: Frozen Berry Jam (page 36).
Back cover: Piccalilli (page 98).

Plum Sauce, page 84

Piccalilli, page 98

All recipes are double-tested by our team of home economists. When we test our recipes, we rate them for ease of preparation. The following cookery ratings are on the recipes in this book, making them easy to use and understand.

A single Cooking with Confidence symbol indicates a recipe that is simple and generally quick to make—perfect for beginners.

Two symbols indicate the need for just a little more care and a little more time.

Three symbols indicate special dishes that need more investment in time, care and patience—but the results are worth it.

IMPORTANT
Those who might be at risk from the effects of salmonella food poisoning (the elderly, pregnant women, young children and those suffering from immune deficiency diseases) should consult their GP with any concerns about eating raw eggs.

Making Jams and Preserves

Imagine eating delectable freshly poached peaches and fresh cherry jam in the middle of winter, or dollops of rich, fruity chutneys with the barbecue in the height of summer. With no previous skills required, preserving is a culinary adventure that can be both satisfying and rewarding.

For centuries, jams, preserves, chutneys and pickles have been made to ensure a regular food supply during colder and leaner times. They are best made during the peak of the season when the fruit and vegetables are plentiful and cheap. Obviously, the use of homegrown produce can save you lots of money, as can buying in bulk from produce markets.

WHICH FRUIT TO CHOOSE

When making jams, preserves, chutneys or pickles it is essential to use good-quality fruits and vegetables to obtain the best results. Always choose fruit that is firm and just ripe, and without any blemishes or bruises. Overripe fruit will lack the pectin needed to set the preserve. If the fruit is quite ripe, add about 10 per cent of underripe fruit to increase the pectin to the amount needed to set the preserve.

SUGAR AND PECTIN

When making jams and jellies the balance of the acid in the fruit, the sugar and the pectin will all play a part in the final firmness and flavour of the preserve. Sugar is not just used as a sweetener when making jams and jellies. It is also a preservative when used in a high concentration, inhibiting the development and growth of micro-organisms. To reach a high enough concentration, 3/4–1 cup of sugar must be used per 1 cup of fruit. Sugar is also a setting agent and aids the setting process in jams and jellies which would not set without a commercial setting agent.

Pectin is found in the skin, flesh and seeds of most fruits in varying degrees. It is particularly high in citrus pith and apple skin. Some fruits are quite low in pectin or have none at all and need the addition of pectin-containing fruit or juice, or commercial setting agents, to help them set.

The acid level of the fruits is also important, because it acts as a preservative and setting agent. If low, acid levels can be supplemented with the addition of lemon juice or by combining several fruits together in a recipe. A commercial setting agent is not always needed and if the preserve sets when tested it may not be necessary to add it at all.

Successful jams and preserves require an even balance of pectin and acid. The chart below describes the levels of pectin and acid found in fruits commonly used in jams and preserves.

TESTING FOR PECTIN

If you are in doubt as to how much pectin is in the fruit you want to use to make your jelly, place 2 teaspoons of methylated spirits in a small bowl and then gently add 1 teaspoon of the strained fruit mixture and stir gently. If there is enough pectin present to set the jelly, clots should form into one large lump. If they form smaller lumps, the mixture will need to be reduced some more or you will need to add some lemon juice. If it is still not setting, you may need to use a commercial setting agent. Follow the instructions on the packet.

SUGAR

You will notice that all our sweet preserve recipes call for warmed sugar. While warming the sugar before adding it to the pan is not absolutely imperative in a recipe and won't affect the final outcome, it does

PECTIN AND ACID LEVELS IN FRUITS

HIGH PECTIN	MEDIUM PECTIN	LOW PECTIN	HIGH ACID	LOW ACID
blackcurrants	apricots	bananas	blackberries	apricots
citrus fruits	blackberries	blackberries	(early)	figs
cooking apples	(early)	(late)	blackcurrants	kiwi fruit
grapes	eating apples	boysenberries	cherries	mangoes
plums	loganberries	cherries	citrus fruits	melons
(some varieties)	mulberries	figs	green apples	passionfruit
quinces	peaches	guava	pineapple	pears
redcurrants	pears	melons	plums	quinces
	raspberries	nectarines	raspberries	rhubarb
	rhubarb	passionfruit	(early)	strawberries
	strawberries	pineapple	redcurrants	sweet apples

Three-fruit Marmalade

speed up the dissolving process. The sugar dissolves more quickly and, being warm, will not reduce the temperature of the fruit mixture as much as if you had added cold sugar. To warm sugar, spread it in an even layer in a deep-sided baking dish and warm in a slow oven 150°C (300°F/ Gas 2) for about 10–15 minutes, or until warmed through. Do not overheat the sugar or it will start to lump together. To make sure, stir the sugar once or twice while it is warming. To save time, warm the sugar while you are cooking the jam.

Do not add the sugar until the fruit has softened. If sugar is added before the fruit is fully soft, it will stay firm. Regular granulated sugar is used in our jam, jelly and preserve recipes unless otherwise specified. Caster sugar is used in some recipes for quicker dissolving and better clarity. Brown sugar is used mostly in chutneys, pickles and relishes to enhance the flavours and give a rich colour.

EQUIPMENT

Large heavy-based stainless steel or enamel pans are one of the most important pieces of equipment you can have when making jams and preserves. You can even buy special preserving pans if you intend to make large amounts.

Sugar thermometers are a very helpful gauge for temperatures. It is crucial, when bottling and sealing your preserve, that the temperature remains at or above 85°C (185°F). This prevents the growth of potentially harmful bacteria. If you don't have a sugar thermometer, make sure you seal your preserve in its jar as soon as it is ready. You can also use your thermometer to test whether your preserve has reached setting point. This generally occurs once the mixture has reached 104°C (220°F). However we haven't used this method much in this book, relying more on testing on a saucer with the wrinkle method. Jam funnels will come in handy and make filling jars a little easier without the jam dripping down the sides. Large and small heatproof jugs are essential for pouring and measuring. A metal skimmer or metal spoon is ideal for removing scum from the surface of the jam or preserve. Ladles are often used to transfer cooked preserves to jars. Wooden spoons are needed for

DEFINITIONS

JAM—made from small pieces of fruit and sugar, cooked to a thick, spreadable consistency.

PRESERVE—whole fruits preserved in a heavy, sugar-based syrup.

CONSERVE—whole or large pieces of fruit cooked with sugar until thick.

JELLY—made from the strained juice of cooked fruits, and sugar. Generally clear, but can contain small pieces of the original fruit.

MARMALADE—sliced, cooked citrus fruits, suspended in a sweet, thick jam mixture.

FRUIT PASTE—sieved, cooked fruit, cooked to a thick paste with sugar and cut into pieces when cold.

FRUIT CURD—thick, spreadable, creamy mixture made with juice, fruit purée, and sometimes citrus rind, combined with sugar, eggs and butter and cooked until thick.

PICKLE—vegetables, or sometimes fruit, pickled in vinegar with sugar, salt and spices.

CHUTNEY—mixture of vegetables and/or fruit cooked with vinegar, sugar and spices to a thick, pulpy consistency.

RELISH—salted cooked vegetables in a sugar, spice and vinegar-based sauce, which is thickened towards the end of cooking.

With just a few basic pieces of equipment, anyone can make jams and preserves.

Roasted Tomato Relish

Always use clean, warm jars to store your jams and preserves.

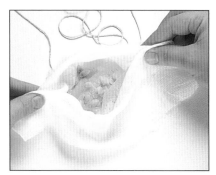

Lemon pips and rind are often added to the cooking mixture in a muslin bag.

HOW IT ALL WORKS

Whether you are making jams, preserves, jellies, pickles, chutneys or relishes, the method is essentially the same. Obviously, sweet jams, preserves and jellies require a lot more sugar than the savoury pickles, chutneys and relishes. They are also self-setting in that the mixture thickens on cooling to an easily spreadable consistency.

JAMS

Try not to cook too much jam all in one quantity. Do not use more than 2 kg (4 lb) fruit in a recipe at a time. You also need to make sure that your pan is large enough. Ideally, the mixture should be no more than 5–6 cm deep after the sugar has been added. Chutneys and pickles can be cooked in larger quantities, but remember that the more mixture you have in the pan, the longer the cooking time. Jellies are generally cooked in smaller quantities.

Wash and dry the fruit well to remove any dirt. If you are using citrus fruits such as oranges or grapefruit, gently scrub the fruit with a soft bristle brush under warm running water to remove the wax coating. Remove any stalks from berries and cut away any damaged or bruised pieces of fruit (which you shouldn't have if you'd chosen your fruit carefully in the beginning!) Cut up the fruit according to the recipe and place it into your pan to soften. Be aware that some recipes require the fruit to be soaked overnight. Reserved seeds and extra skin or fruit are used in many recipes in this book, particularly lemon pips and rind. These are wrapped in a square of muslin and can either be soaked overnight with the fruit, and then cooked with the fruit, as in the case of marmalade, or simply added to the pan and cooked with the jam or preserve. For easy retrieval of the muslin bag, attach a long piece of string to the bag and tie it to the handle of the pan. The remaining ingredients are added according to each individual recipe.

Bring the mixture to the boil, then reduce the heat and simmer for the specified time until the fruit is tender,

stirring, and, of course, a pastry brush to clean down the sides of the pan.

Muslin is used throughout this book both to drain liquids and to hold seeds and rind in a secure bundle. Muslin can be purchased at kitchenware or fabric stores. Alternatively, you can use a clean tea towel. When straining mixtures such as jellies, ensure the material is just damp so it won't absorb too much of the liquid.

Before starting to cook your jam or preserve, ensure your equipment has been carefully washed in hot, soapy water and the jars you intend to use are thoroughly clean. Always make sure you have enough clean jars ready for when you have a pan full of boiling jam ready to bottle. The best way to ensure that the jars are spotlessly clean is to preheat the oven to very slow 120°C (250°F/Gas 1/2). Thoroughly wash the jars and lids in hot, soapy water (or preferably in a dishwasher) and rinse well with hot water. Put the jars onto the baking trays and place them in the oven for 20 minutes, or until you are ready to use them. Dry them fully in the oven.

STICKY SITUATIONS

CRYSTALLIZATION—too much sugar was added to the fruit, and it was not dissolved properly before boiling.

TOUGH FRUIT—the fruit was not cooked long enough before the sugar was added. Fruit does not soften any further once sugar is added.

FRUIT FLOATS—the fruit was not cooked long enough or did not stand long enough before bottling.

TOO RUNNY—the mixture has not set properly. Return it to the pan, bring to the boil again and retest for setting point before bottling.

MOULD—can start to grow once the jar is opened if storing in a warm place, or if the mixture was not covered while hot. If caught quickly, mould can be scooped off with a little jam and discarded. Refrigerate the remainder and eat as soon as possible.

FERMENTATION—mushy, overripe, bruised or damaged fruit were used in the cooking process, or not enough sugar was added to the fruit mixture. If you do use less sugar in a recipe, make sure you eat it within a few months because it won't keep as long. The set won't be quite as firm. Keep in the refrigerator after opening

CLOUDINESS—this generally only occurs in jellies, when the jelly bag was squeezed or disturbed while the fruit was dripping through.

then add the required amount of sugar. Remove any scum or foam from the top of the jam or preserve all through the cooking process. The scum that forms on the top of the mixture is usually any impurities or dirt on the fruit or sugar. Stir over heat, without boiling, until all the sugar has dissolved. Brush the side of the pan with a pastry brush dipped in water, to dissolve any excess sugar crystals which can sometimes cause

jams to crystallize towards the end of cooking. If the jam does crystallize, add 1–2 tablespoons of lemon juice and gently reheat. Be aware that this may change the taste slightly.

Once all the sugar has dissolved, boil the mixture rapidly for the required time. Stir the jam often while it is cooking to speed up the cooking process and ensure that it does not stick to the bottom of the pan.

After the specified cooking time is completed, or when the jam or preserve looks thick and syrupy, the mixture should fall from a wooden spoon heavily with 3 or 4 drops joining together as they drop. This means that the jam or preserve has reached its setting point.

Cooking times vary greatly between recipes, depending on pan sizes, the fruit used, the time of year, if the fruit is in season, etc. Therefore, it is necessary to test for setting point, sometimes up to 10 minutes before the stated time, to make sure the jam or preserve is ready to be bottled. Do not rely entirely on the times stated. Remove the pan from the heat, place 1 teaspoon of the jam onto one of the cold plates and place it in the freezer for about 30 seconds, or until the jam has cooled to room temperature. Gently push through the jam with the tip of your finger. There should be a skin on top of the jam which should wrinkle. If it does wrinkle, it's ready. Ta da!! If not, return the mixture briefly to the heat and try again in a few minutes with the second plate.

Immediately spoon or pour the mixture into the warm, clean jars. Pulpier jams tend to have a thicker consistency and jams with large pieces of fruit will need a few minutes standing in the pan before bottling to allow the fruit to be evenly suspended in the mixture. Don't leave the jam or jelly for too long or it will start to set in the pan. If this does happen, you will need to start all over again. Take care when pouring the preserves into the jars as the mixture is extremely hot. Hold the jar in a tea towel and pour or spoon in the preserve, filling right to the top. If your jars have small openings it may be easier to pour the jam into a clean heatproof jug first and then into the jars. You can also use a jam funnel.

Scum should be removed from the surface during cooking.

Brush the side of the pan with a wet pastry brush to remove any sugar crystals.

Setting point has been reached when the jam drops from a spoon in thick sheets.

Use clean, thin metal skewers to remove air bubbles from the jars before sealing.

If the jam has not reached setting point, it will not wrinkle when tested.

The wrinkle test is a quick and easy way to see if jam has reached its setting point.

If the jam is overcooked, it is much thicker and darker than it should be.

The fruit mixture must drip through the jelly bag undisturbed, or the jelly will cloud.

Rosemary Wine Jelly

Occasionally, you will find you have air bubbles in the bottles. To remove them, use a thin clean skewer to help push the mixture to the side and release the bubble to the surface. This technique can be used for all types of preserves. Alternatively, a gentle tap on a cloth on the bench will release some of the air bubbles. Seal the jars while the mixture is still hot. Turn the jars upside down for 2 minutes, then invert and leave to cool. This will ensure the fruit is evenly distributed and the lids are sterilized.

JELLIES
Choose fruits with a good pectin and acid balance for the best results. The fruit is cooked with or without water and then strained overnight in a damp jelly bag (these are available in good kitchenware stores) or damp muslin bag suspended over a stool. A wide bowl is placed underneath to catch the liquid. Don't squeeze the jelly bag or the liquid and resulting jelly will turn cloudy. You can use the pectin test if necessary, but the recipes in this book give you the required amount of sugar for the fruit used. Add the sugar, stir until dissolved and then boil rapidly for the required time, following the same method for jams. Skimming off the scum is essential at this stage or it will make the jelly cloudy later on. Before pouring into the clean, warm jars, allow any bubbles in the pan to subside. Pour the jelly down the sides of the jars to prevent any bubbles forming.

SAVOURY PRESERVES
All the basics of jam making apply when cooking savoury preserves as

well. Generally, they are cooked until thick and pulpy, not watery, and when tested on a plate will leave a clean trail behind without any runny liquid. Choose firm, ripe and unblemished vegetables. Always use clean, warm jars and equipment, and refrigerate the preserve after opening.

Savoury preserves contain a variety of herbs and spices. It is important to remember that dried herbs and spices do lose their flavour if kept too long and this can affect the final flavour of your preserve. It is best to buy in small, rather than large, quantities.

Testing for flavour while the preserve is hot doesn't always give a true indication of the final flavour. The flavours will only develop fully after a few weeks' storage. For a quick idea of the taste, allow a little to cool on a saucer before trying it. Ideally, before making changes to a recipe and adding new flavours, it is best to make the recipe first as stated in the book. After storage, taste the preserve and then decide what changes you would like to make the next time you cook it.

CHUTNEYS
Long, slow cooking of both vegetables and fruit, with the addition of sugar, vinegar and spices so that the flavours and colours are both rich and concentrated, produce a thick, flavoursome pulp known as chutney. The flavour variations seem endless, depending on the fruit and vegetables used and the spices added.

Spices play a large part in chutney making and can change a plain chutney into a deliciously spicy aromatic one with the addition of chillies, cardamom and cinnamon, to name just a few. Just be careful not to add too many or you will overpower the flavours of the fruit in the chutney. Chutneys are cooked until very thick. They must be stirred often to prevent sticking and burning on the bottom of the pan. When tested on a plate, they should leave a clean trail behind without any runny liquid.

PICKLES
Preparing vegetables for pickling involves soaking them in a brine (salt and water solution) or layering them sprinkled with salt for 24 hours. The salt draws out moisture from the vegetables, which softens them and removes any excess liquid which may dilute the vinegar. It also adds to the final flavour. The vegetables should be rinsed well under cold running water after salting. They can be left raw or lightly cooked and are packed into clean jars and topped with a vinegar solution. Spices can also be added to increase the flavour.

RELISHES
The method for making relishes is very similar to that for making pickles. First salt the vegetables, then rinse them under cold, running water. The vegetable mixture is then simmered in a spicy vinegar solution before being thickened with cornflour or a slurry—a thin paste made from plain flour and water.

CURDS
Gently cooked over a pan of simmering water, curds still require that the basics of jam making are followed. The combination of egg and butter thickens the fruit mixture both during cooking and once refrigerated.

FRUIT PASTES
Fruit pastes are a cross between jelly and jam. It is a sieved fruit purée, cooked with sugar until thick and paste like. Again the basics of jam making apply here, and great care is needed to avoid being splattered with the thick mixture as it bubbles like hot lava in the base of the pan. Take care not to overcook it or let the mixture catch and burn on the bottom. Fruit pastes use a large amount of fruit, so it is best to make them when there is an overabundance.

STORAGE TIMES

JAMS, CONSERVES, PRESERVES
Store in an airtight jar in a cool, dark place for 6–12 months. Once opened, store in the refrigerator for 6 weeks.

JELLIES
Store in an airtight jar in a cool, dark place for 6–12 months. Once opened, store in the refrigerator for 1 month.

CURDS
Store in an airtight jar in the refrigerator for up to 2 weeks.

FRUIT PASTES
Set in disposable foil trays or wrap in greaseproof paper, then plastic wrap, then foil and then plastic wrap again. Store in a cool, dark place for 6–12 months.

SAUCES, CHUTNEYS, RELISHES AND PICKLES
Sauces, chutneys, relishes and pickles should be left for 1 month before eating to allow the flavours to develop. Store in a cool, dark place for up to 1 year. Once opened, store refrigerated for 6 weeks.

HEAT-PROCESSED FRUITS AND VEGETABLES
Store in a cool, dark place for up to 1 year. Once opened, store in the refrigerator for 1 week.

MUSTARDS
Store in a cool, dark place for up to 3 months. Once opened, refrigerate for 1–2 weeks.

When tested, the chutney should leave a clean trail without any runny liquid.

Curds are made of fruit, egg and butter and reach a thick, creamy consistency.

SWEET JAMS AND PRESERVES

STRAWBERRY JAM

Preparation time: 15 minutes
Total cooking time: 1 hour
Makes 1.5 litres (48 fl oz)

1.5 kg (3 lb) strawberries
**¹/₂ cup (125 ml/4 fl oz) lemon
    juice**
**1.25 kg (2 lb 8 oz) sugar,
    warmed (see page 5)**

1 Put two small plates in the freezer. Wipe the strawberries clean and hull them. Place the strawberries in a large pan with the lemon juice, warmed sugar and ¹/₂ cup (125 ml/4 fl oz) water. Warm gently, without boiling, stirring carefully with a wooden spoon. Try not to break up the berries too much.
2 Increase the heat and, without boiling, continue to stir the mixture for 10 minutes, or until all the sugar has dissolved. Increase the heat and boil for 20 minutes, stirring often. Skim any scum off the surface with a skimmer or slotted spoon. Start testing for setting point after 20 minutes, but it may take up to 40 minutes. Be careful that the jam does not catch on the base of the pan and start to burn.
3 Remove from the heat, place a little jam onto one of the cold plates and place in the freezer for 30 seconds. When setting point is reached, a skin will form on the surface and the jam will wrinkle when pushed with your finger. Remove any scum from the surface.
4 Spoon immediately into clean, warm jars and seal. Turn the jars upside down for 2 minutes, then invert and leave to cool. Label and date. Store in a cool, dark place for 6–12 months. Refrigerate after opening for up to 6 weeks.

COOK'S FILE

Note: Do not wash strawberries once they have been hulled. They will absorb water and the taste will be affected.

Skim any scum off the surface with a skimmer or slotted spoon.

When setting point is reached, the jam will wrinkle when pushed with your finger.

REDCURRANT JELLY

Preparation time: 20 minutes
Total cooking time: 20 minutes
Makes 2 cups (500 ml/16 fl oz)

600 g (1¼ lb) redcurrants
2⅓ cups (590 g/1 lb 3 oz)
   caster sugar, warmed
   (see page 5)

1 Put two small plates in the freezer. Place the redcurrants, including stems, and sugar in a pan. Crush the redcurrants to release the juices. Cook, stirring, over low heat, until all the sugar has dissolved.

2 Increase the heat and boil rapidly for 5 minutes, stirring often. Remove from the heat, place a little jelly onto one of the cold plates and place in the freezer for 30 seconds. When setting point is reached, a skin will form on the surface and the jelly will wrinkle when pushed with your finger. Skim off any scum with a skimmer or slotted spoon and push the mixture through a fine sieve into a heatproof jug.

3 Pour immediately into clean, warm jars and seal. Turn upside down for 2 minutes, then invert and leave to cool. Label and date. Store in a cool, dark place for 6–12 months. Refrigerate after opening for up to 6 weeks.

COOK'S FILE

Note: For a shiny glaze and beautiful finish on sweet fruit tarts, melt a little jelly with water and brush over the top of the fruit. Or melt a spoonful in savoury sauces and gravies.

Crush the redcurrants with a large spoon or potato masher to release the juices.

Push the mixture through a fine sieve into a heatproof jug.

Pour the jelly from the heatproof jug into clean, warm jars and seal.

DUNDEE MARMALADE

Preparation time: 1 hour 30 minutes +
 overnight soaking
Total cooking time: 1 hour 20 minutes
Makes 3.25 litres (104 fl oz)

1.5 kg (3 lb) Seville oranges
2 lemons
1.5 kg (3 lb) sugar, warmed
 (see page 5)
3³/₄ cups (700 g/1 lb 6¹/₂ oz)
 soft brown sugar
2 tablespoons treacle
2 tablespoons whisky, optional

1 Scrub the fruit under warm, running water with a soft bristle brush to remove the wax coating. Cut the fruit in half, then cut each half into quarters. Slice thinly, removing and retaining the pips. Place the pips on a square of muslin and tie securely with string. Place the fruit and muslin bag in a large non-metal bowl. Pour in 7 cups (1.75 litres/56 fl oz) water, cover with plastic wrap and leave overnight.

2 Put two small plates in the freezer. Place the fruit and muslin bag in a large pan. Bring to the boil, then reduce the heat and simmer, covered, for 45 minutes, or until the fruit is tender.

3 Add the sugars and treacle. Stir the mixture over low heat, without boiling, for 5 minutes, or until all the sugar has dissolved. Return to the boil and boil rapidly for 30 minutes, stirring often. Remove any scum from the surface during cooking with a skimmer or slotted spoon. When the marmalade falls from a tilted wooden spoon in thick sheets without dripping, start testing for setting point.

4 Remove from the heat, place a little marmalade onto one of the cold plates and place in the freezer for 30 seconds. When setting point is reached, a skin will form on the surface and the marmalade will wrinkle when pushed with your finger. Discard the muslin bag. Remove any scum from the surface. Stir in the whisky.

5 Spoon immediately into clean, warm jars and seal. Turn upside down for 2 minutes, then invert and leave to cool. Label and date. Store in a cool, dark place for 6–12 months. Refrigerate after opening for up to 6 weeks.

Cut the oranges and lemons in half, and then each half into quarters.

Put the orange and lemon pips on a piece of muslin and tie with string.

When the setting point is reached, the marmalade will wrinkle when pushed.

FIG PRESERVE

Preparation time: 20 minutes
Total cooking time: 45 minutes
Makes 1 litre (32 fl oz)

1 kg (2 lb) fresh figs, stalks removed
1/2 cup (125 ml/4 fl oz) lemon juice
1 kg (2 lb) sugar, warmed (see page 5)

1 Put two small plates in the freezer. Put the figs in a large heatproof bowl. Cover with boiling water for 3 minutes. Drain, cool and cut into pieces.

2 Place the figs, lemon juice and 1/2 cup (125 ml/4 fl oz) water in a large pan. Bring to the boil, then reduce the heat and simmer, covered, for 20 minutes, or until the figs are soft.

3 Add the sugar and stir over medium heat, without boiling, for 5 minutes, or until all the sugar has dissolved.

4 Bring to the boil and boil for 20 minutes, stirring often. Remove any scum from the surface during cooking with a skimmer or slotted spoon. Add a little water if the mixture thickens too much. When thick and pulpy, start testing for setting point.

5 Remove from the heat, place a little preserve onto one of the cold plates and place in the freezer for 30 seconds. When setting point is reached, a skin will form on the surface and the preserve will wrinkle when pushed with your finger. Remove any scum from the surface.

6 Pour immediately into clean, warm jars, and seal. Turn the jars upside down for 2 minutes, then invert and leave to cool. Label and date. Store in a cool, dark place for 6–12 months. Refrigerate after opening for up to 6 weeks.

Place the chopped figs in a pan with the water and lemon juice.

Start testing for setting point when the jam is thick and pulpy.

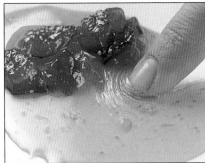

The jam will wrinkle when pushed with your finger when setting point is reached.

MIXED BERRY JAM

Preparation time: 20 minutes
Total cooking time: 35 minutes
Makes 1.25 litres (40 fl oz)

1 kg (2 lb) berries (strawberries,
  raspberries, blackberries,
  blueberries, mulberries)
⅓ cup (80 ml/2¾ fl oz) lemon juice
1 kg (2 lb) sugar, warmed
  (see page 5)
25 g (¾ oz) jam setting mixture

1 Place the berries and lemon juice in a large pan and gently cook for 10 minutes. Add the sugar and stir over low heat for 5 minutes, or until all the sugar has dissolved.
2 Boil for 15 minutes, stirring often, and then remove from the heat. Add the jam setting mixture, then return the berry mixture to the heat and boil rapidly for a further 5 minutes. Remove any scum from the surface with a skimmer or slotted spoon.
3 Pour immediately into clean, warm jars, and seal. Turn the jars upside down for 2 minutes, then invert and leave to cool. Label and date. Store in a cool, dark place for 6–12 months. Refrigerate after opening for up to 6 weeks.

COOK'S FILE

Note: Remove the stems, stalks, leaves and any blemishes from the berries you have chosen. If the berries are sandy or gritty, wash them gently under cold water and drain well in a colander before use. You can use a mixture of fresh and frozen berries, if necessary.

Add the jam setting mixture before returning to the boil for 5 minutes.

Remove any scum from the surface with a skimmer or slotted spoon.

Turn the jars upside down for 2 minutes, before inverting and leaving to cool.

MICROWAVE JAMS

These recipes are based on an 850 watt microwave. If your microwave wattage is different, cooking times may vary. Take extra care when cooking jams in a microwave, due to the extreme heat.

STRAWBERRY JAM

Put two small plates in the freezer. Hull and quarter 750 g (1¹/2 lb) fresh strawberries, place in a microwave-proof bowl with ¹/4 cup (60 ml/2 fl oz) lemon juice. Place the white pith from 1 lemon onto a square of muslin, tie securely with string and place in the bowl. Cook, uncovered, on high for 6 minutes, or until the mixture is soft and pulpy, stirring once or twice. Cool slightly then measure. Add 1 cup (250 g/8 oz) sugar for every cup of fruit mixture and stir until the sugar has dissolved. Cook, uncovered, on high for 15–20 minutes, or until the mixture reaches setting point. Test for setting point a couple of times during cooking (see page 7). Discard the muslin bag. Carefully pour the very hot (85°C) jam into clean, warm jars and seal. Turn the jars upside down for 2 minutes, then invert and leave to cool. Label and date.
Makes 2 cups (500 ml/16 fl oz)

DRIED FIG JAM

Put two small plates in the freezer. Remove the stalks from 500 g (1 lb) dried figs and place in a microwave-proof bowl with 1¹/2 cups (375 ml/12 fl oz) water and 2 tablespoons lemon juice. Place the white pith from 1 lemon onto a square of muslin, tie securely with string and place in the bowl. Cook, uncovered, on high for 10 minutes, or until the mixture is soft and pulpy, stirring once or twice. Cool slightly then measure. Add 1 cup (250 g/8 oz) sugar for every cup of fruit mixture and stir until all the sugar has dissolved. Cook, uncovered, on high for 15–20 minutes, or until the mixture reaches setting point. Test for setting point a couple of times during cooking (see page 7). Discard the muslin bag. Carefully pour the very hot (85°C) jam into clean, warm jars. Turn the jars upside down for 2 minutes, then invert and leave to cool. Label and date.
Makes 1 litre (32 fl oz)

CITRUS MARMALADE

Put two small plates in the freezer. Remove the rind from a grapefruit, a lemon and an orange. Remove the pith and roughly chop the flesh. Remove the seeds. Place the pith and seeds onto a square of muslin and tie securely with string. Place the rind and muslin bag in a microwave-proof bowl and cover with 1¹/2 cups (375 ml/12 fl oz) water. Cook, uncovered, on high for 10 minutes, or until the rind is soft. Cool slightly, then measure. Add 1 cup (250 g/8 oz) sugar for every cup of the fruit mixture and stir until dissolved. Cook, uncovered, on high for 20–25 minutes, or until the mixture reaches setting point. Test for setting point a couple of times during cooking (see page 7). Discard the muslin bag. Carefully pour the very hot (85°C) jam into clean, warm jars. Turn the jars upside down for 2 minutes, then invert and leave to cool. Label and date.
Makes 2 cups (500 ml/16 fl oz)

APRICOT JAM

Put two small plates in the freezer. Halve and remove the stones from 500 g (1 lb) fresh apricots and roughly chop. Place in a microwave-proof bowl with 2 tablespoons lemon juice. Place the white pith from 1 lemon onto a square of muslin, tie securely with string and place in the bowl. Cook, uncovered, on high for 6 minutes, stirring once or twice. Cool slightly, then measure. Add 1 cup (250 g/8 oz) sugar for every cup of fruit mixture and stir until all the sugar has dissolved. Cook, uncovered, on high for 15–20 minutes, or until the mixture reaches setting point. Test for setting point a couple of times during cooking (see page 7). Discard the muslin bag. Carefully pour the very hot (85°C) jam into clean, warm jars. Turn the jars upside down for 2 minutes, then invert and leave to cool. Label and date.
Makes 2 cups (500 ml/16 fl oz)

MIXED BERRY JAM

Put two small plates in the freezer. Place 500 g (1 lb) mixed berries in a microwave-proof bowl with ¹/4 cup (60 ml/2 fl oz) lemon juice. Place the white pith from 1 lemon onto a square of muslin, tie securely with string and place in the bowl. Cook, uncovered, on high for 6 minutes or until the mixture is soft and pulpy, stirring once or twice. Cool slightly then measure. Add 1 cup (250 g/8 oz) sugar for every cup of fruit mixture and stir until all the sugar has dissolved. Cook, uncovered, on high for 15–20 minutes, or until the mixture reaches setting point. Test for setting point a couple of times during cooking (see page 7). Discard the muslin bag. Carefully pour the very hot (85°C) jam into clean, warm jars. Turn the jars upside down for 2 minutes, then invert and leave to cool. Label and date.
Makes 2 cups (500 ml/16 fl oz)

RASPBERRY JAM

Put two small plates in the freezer. Place 500 g (1 lb) raspberries in a microwave-proof bowl with ¹/4 cup (60 ml/2 fl oz) lemon juice. Place the white pith from 1 lemon onto a square of muslin, tie securely with string and place in the bowl. Cook, uncovered, on high for 6 minutes, or until the mixture is soft and pulpy, stirring once or twice. Cool slightly and then measure. Add 1 cup (250 g/8 oz) sugar for every cup of fruit mixture and stir until all the sugar has dissolved. Cook, uncovered, on high for 15–20 minutes, or until the mixture reaches setting point. Test for setting point a couple of times during cooking (see page 7). Discard the muslin bag. Carefully pour the very hot (85°C) jam into clean, warm jars. Turn the jars upside down for 2 minutes, then invert and leave to cool. Label and date. Makes 2 cups (500 ml/16 fl oz)

Clockwise from top left: Apricot jam; citrus marmalade; strawberry jam; raspberry jam; mixed berry jam; fig jam.

APRICOT AND PASSIONFRUIT JAM

Preparation time: 15 minutes
Total cooking time: 45 minutes
Makes 1.25 litres (40 fl oz)

1.2 kg (2 lb 6¹/2 oz) fresh
   apricots, stones removed
1 kg (2 lb) sugar, warmed
   (see page 5)
²/3 cup (160 g/5¹/2 oz)
   passionfruit pulp
2 tablespoons lemon juice

1 Put two small plates in the freezer. Cut the apricots into quarters and place in a large pan with ¹/3 cup (80 ml/ 2³/4 fl oz) water. Cover and cook over low heat for 10 minutes, or until tender.
2 Remove from the heat and add the sugar, passionfruit pulp and lemon juice. Heat slowly, stirring, for 5 minutes, or until all the sugar has dissolved. Return to the boil and boil rapidly for 30 minutes, stirring often. Remove any scum during cooking with a skimmer or slotted spoon. When the jam falls from a tilted wooden spoon in thick sheets without dripping, start testing for setting point.
3 Remove from the heat, place a little jam onto one of the cold plates and place in the freezer for 30 seconds. When setting point is reached, a skin will form on the surface and the jam will wrinkle when pushed with your finger. Remove any scum from the surface.
4 Spoon immediately into clean, warm jars and seal. Turn the jars upside down for 2 minutes, then invert and leave to cool. Label and date. Store in a cool, dark place for 6–12 months. Refrigerate after opening for up to 6 weeks.

Cook the apricots gently for 10 minutes, or until they are tender.

Start testing for setting point when the jam falls from a wooden spoon in thick sheets.

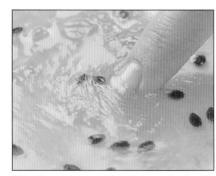

The jam will wrinkle when pushed with your finger when setting point is reached.

RASPBERRY JAM

Preparation time: 10 minutes
Total cooking time: 35 minutes
Makes 2 litres (64 fl oz)

1.5 kg (3 lb) fresh or frozen
   raspberries
1/3 cup (80 ml/2¾ fl oz) lemon juice
1.5 kg (3 lb) sugar, warmed
   (see page 5)

1 Place two plates in the freezer. Place the berries and lemon juice in a large pan. Stir over low heat for 10 minutes, or until the berries are soft.
2 Add the sugar and stir, without boiling, for 5 minutes, or until all the sugar has dissolved.
3 Bring the mixture to the boil and boil, for 20 minutes. Stir often and make sure the jam doesn't stick or burn on the base of the pan. Remove any scum during cooking with a skimmer or slotted spoon. When the jam falls from a tilted wooden spoon in thick sheets without dripping, start testing for setting point.
4 Remove from the heat, place a little jam onto one of the cold plates and place in the freezer for 30 seconds. When setting point is reached, a skin will form on the surface and the jam will wrinkle when pushed with your finger. Remove any scum.
5 Spoon immediately into clean, warm jars and seal. Turn the jars upside down for 2 minutes, then invert and leave to cool. Label and date. Store in a cool, dark place for 6–12 months. Refrigerate after opening for up to 6 weeks.

COOK'S FILE

Note: Frozen raspberries can be used, but the cooking time will increase.

Add the warmed sugar to the softened raspberry mixture.

Skim any scum from the surface with a skimmer or slotted spoon.

A skin forms on the surface and the jam wrinkles when setting point is reached.

BLUEBERRY PRESERVE

Preparation time: 10 minutes
Total cooking time: 35 minutes
Makes 1 litre (32 fl oz)

1 kg (2 lb) blueberries
1/4 cup (60 ml/2 fl oz) lemon juice
    (and the pips of 1 lemon)
1 kg (2 lb) sugar, warmed
    (see page 5)

1 Put two small plates in the freezer. Place the berries in a large pan with 3/4 cup (185 ml/6 fl oz) water. Place the lemon pips onto a piece of muslin and tie securely with string. Add to the pan. Cook over low heat for 5 minutes, or until the berries just start to colour the water.

2 Add the lemon juice and sugar, and stir over low heat for 5 minutes, or until all the sugar has dissolved. Bring slowly to the boil and cook for 20–25 minutes, stirring often. Remove any scum during cooking with a skimmer or slotted spoon. When the preserve falls from a tilted wooden spoon in thick sheets without dripping, start testing for setting point.

3 Remove from the heat, place a little preserve onto one of the cold plates and place in the freezer for 30 seconds. When setting point is reached, a skin will form on the surface and the preserve will wrinkle when pushed with your finger. Remove any scum from the surface.

4 Transfer to a heatproof jug and pour immediately into clean, warm jars and seal. Turn the jars upside down for 2 minutes, then invert and leave to cool. Label and date. Store in a cool, dark place for 6–12 months. Refrigerate after opening for up to 6 weeks.

Place the lemon pips onto a square of muslin and tie securely with string.

The jam will wrinkle when pushed with your finger when setting point is reached.

Using a heatproof jug, pour the preserve into clean, warm jars.

PEACH CONSERVE

Preparation time: 20 minutes
Total cooking time: 1 hour 5 minutes
Makes 1.25 litres (40 fl oz)

**1.5 kg (3 lb) peaches (about
    9 large peaches)
1 green apple
1 lemon
1 kg (2 lb) sugar, warmed
    (see page 5)**

1 Put two small plates in the freezer. Score a cross in the base of the peaches. Place them in a large heatproof bowl and cover with boiling water. Leave for 1–2 minutes, then remove with a slotted spoon, cool slightly and peel. Halve, remove the stone and chop into 2 cm (1 inch) pieces.

2 Chop the apple, including the peel and core, into 1 cm ($1/2$ inch) pieces. Peel thin strips of rind from the lemon, then cut it in half and juice. Place the apple and lemon rind onto a square of muslin and tie securely with string.

3 Place the chopped peaches, muslin bag and $1^1/4$ cups (310 ml/10 fl oz) water into a large pan. Bring slowly to the boil, then reduce the heat and simmer for 30 minutes, or until the peaches are tender. Remove any scum from the surface during cooking with a skimmer or slotted spoon. Squeeze any excess juice from the muslin bag by pushing firmly against the side of the pan, then discard the bag.

4 Add the sugar and stir over low heat for 5 minutes, or until all the sugar has dissolved. Add the lemon juice, return to the boil and boil rapidly for 30 minutes, stirring often. Stir across the base of the pan to check that the conserve is not sticking or burning.

When the conserve falls from a tilted wooden spoon in thick sheets without dripping, start testing for setting point.
5 Remove from the heat, place a little conserve onto one of the cold plates and place in the freezer for 30 seconds. When setting point is reached, a skin will form on the surface and the conserve will wrinkle when pushed with your finger. Remove any scum from the surface.

6 Spoon immediately into clean, warm jars and seal. Turn the jars upside down for 2 minutes, then invert and leave to cool. Label and date. Store in a cool, dark place for 6–12 months. Refrigerate after opening for up to 6 weeks.

Score a cross in the base of the peaches, cover in boiling water, cool and peel.

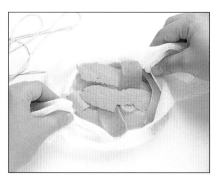

Make a muslin bag containing the apple and lemon rind and tie with string.

Remove any excess juice from the muslin bag by pushing against the side of the pan.

TOMATO AND PINEAPPLE JAM

Preparation time: 20 minutes
Total cooking time: 35 minutes
Makes 2 litres (64 fl oz)

3 kg (6 lb) ripe tomatoes
2.25 kg (4¹/2 lb) sugar, warmed
    (see page 5)
¹/2 cup (125 ml/4 fl oz)
    lemon juice
440 g (14 oz) can crushed
    pineapple

1 Put two small plates in the freezer. Cut a cross in the base of the tomatoes, place in a large bowl, cover with boiling water and leave for 30 seconds, or until the skins start to spilt. Transfer the tomatoes to a bowl of cold water. Remove the skin and chop the tomatoes.

2 Place the tomato in a large pan. Add half the warmed sugar and simmer for 5–10 minutes over low heat, stirring, until the tomato has softened and all the sugar has dissolved.

3 Add the lemon juice, pineapple and remaining sugar. Stir over low heat until all the sugar has dissolved. Bring to the boil and cook for 20–25 minutes, stirring frequently. Remove any scum from the surface during cooking with a skimmer or slotted spoon. When the jam falls from a tilted wooden spoon in thick sheets without dripping, start testing for setting point.

4 Remove from the heat, place a little jam onto one of the cold plates and place in the freezer for 30 seconds. When setting point is reached, a skin will form on the surface and the jam will wrinkle when pushed with your finger. Remove any scum from the surface.

5 Spoon immediately into clean, warm jars and seal. Turn the jars upside down for 2 minutes, then invert and leave to cool. Label and date. Store in a cool, dark place for 6–12 months. Refrigerate after opening for up to 6 weeks.

COOK'S FILE

Note: Ensure the tomatoes are very ripe to maximise the taste of your jam. Vine-ripened tomatoes generally have the best flavour, however, they are also the most expensive.

Simmer the peeled, chopped tomatoes for 5–10 minutes, or until softened.

The jam will wrinkle when pushed with your finger when setting point is reached.

BLOOD PLUM JAM

Preparation time: 20 minutes
Total cooking time: 1 hour 15 minutes
Makes 2 litres (64 fl oz)

2 kg (4 lb) blood plums
1/2 cup (125 ml/4 fl oz) lemon
**   juice**
1.5 kg (3 lb) sugar, warmed
**   (see page 5)**

1 Put two small plates in the freezer. Cut the plums in half and remove the stones. Place in a large pan and add 1 litre (32 fl oz) water. Bring slowly to the boil, then reduce the heat and simmer, covered, for 50 minutes, or until the fruit is soft.
2 Add the lemon juice and sugar and stir over low heat, without boiling, for 5 minutes, or until all the sugar has dissolved. Bring to the boil and boil for 20 minutes, stirring often. Remove any scum from the surface during cooking with a skimmer or slotted spoon. When the jam falls from a tilted wooden spoon in thick sheets without dripping, start testing for setting point.
3 Remove from the heat, place a little jam onto one of the cold plates and place in the freezer for 30 seconds. When setting point is reached, a skin will form on the surface and the jam will wrinkle when pushed with your finger. Remove any scum from the surface.
4 Spoon immediately into clean, warm jars and seal. Turn the jars upside down for 2 minutes, then invert and leave to cool. Label and date. Store in a cool, dark place for 6–12 months. Refrigerate after opening for up to 6 weeks.

COOK'S FILE

Note: Blood plums have dark skin and dark flesh. If they are not available, any kind of plum can be used.

Halve the plums and remove the stones before cooking.

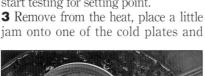
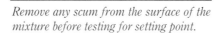

Remove any scum from the surface of the mixture before testing for setting point.

The jam will wrinkle when pushed with your finger when setting point is reached.

LIQUEUR FRUITS

Served over ice cream, with ricotta cheese or mascarpone, with brioche or panettone, or over toasted waffles or crêpes, these luscious, decadent liqueur fruits make an ideal finale to any meal. Make sure the fruit you use is just ripe and free of blemishes. Liqueur fruits should be left for a month before using to allow the flavours to develop and must be refrigerated after opening. Make sure the jars have an airtight seal, otherwise the fruit may spoil. What a waste!

APRICOTS IN RUM

Place 3/4 cup (185 g/6 oz) sugar in a pan with 2 cups (500 ml/16 fl oz) water. Stir over low heat until the sugar has dissolved. Bring to the boil, add 500 g (1 lb) dried apricots, reduce the heat and simmer for 3 minutes. Remove the pan from the heat and stir in 3/4 cup (185 ml/6 fl oz) dark rum. Make sure the temperature is at least 85°C and spoon into a clean, warm 1 litre (32 fl oz) jar. Seal while hot and leave to cool. Label and date. Leave for 1 month before using. Store in a cool, dry place for 6 months. Makes 1 litre (32 fl oz)
Note: It is very important to use a good-quality rum for this recipe as it will drastically affect the flavour.

PRUNES IN PORT

Place 1/2 cup (125 ml/4 fl oz) water, 1/3 cup (90 g/3 oz) sugar and 8 cloves into a large pan. Stir over low heat until the sugar has dissolved. Bring to the boil, then reduce the heat and simmer for 15 minutes. Add 600 g (11/4 lb) pitted prunes, the thinly sliced rind of 1 orange and about 2 cups (500 ml/16 fl oz) port. Make sure the temperature is at least 85°C and spoon into a 1 litre (32 fl oz) clean, warm jar. Seal while hot and leave to cool. Label and date. Leave for 1 month before using. Store in a cool, dry place for 6 months. Makes 1 litre (32 fl oz)
Note: The prunes will swell during standing.

PRESERVED FIGS IN BRANDY

Place 3 cups (750 g/11/2 lb) sugar in a pan with 11/2 cups (375 ml/12 fl oz) water. Stir over low heat until all the sugar has dissolved. Bring to the boil, then reduce the heat, add 400 g (13 oz) firm fresh figs and simmer for 5 minutes, or until the figs begin to soften (this will depend on the ripeness of the figs). Lift the figs from the syrup with a slotted spoon, allowing as much syrup as possible to drain off and place them in clean, warm, wide-neck jars. Repeat with the remaining figs. Gently shake the jars to help settle the figs. Some syrup will accumulate in the jars, so place the slotted spoon over the mouth of the jars and tip the excess syrup back into the pan. Bring the syrup to the boil and boil for 10 minutes, or until it thickens. Remove from the heat, allow any bubbles to subside and pour 11/2 cups (375 ml/12 fl oz) of the syrup into a large heatproof jug, reserving any remaining syrup. Stir in 11/2 cups (375 ml/12 fl oz) brandy and pour into the jars to cover the figs. If there is not enough brandy syrup to cover, combine small quantities of the reserved syrup and some of the brandy in a jug and cover the figs. Make sure the temperature is at least 85°C and seal while hot. Label and store for 1 month before using. Store in a cool, dry place for 6 months. Refrigerate after opening. Makes 1 litre (32 fl oz)

MUSCAT FRUITS

Place 150 g (5 oz) prunes, 150 g (5 oz) small dried figs, stems removed, 100 g (31/2 oz) dried sliced apples, 100 g (31/2 oz) dried peach halves, 100 g (31/2 oz) dried apricot halves, 100 g (31/2 oz) raisins, 2 strips orange rind, 2 cinnamon sticks, halved, 4 whole cloves and 3 cups (750 ml/24 fl oz) clear apple juice in a large non-metallic bowl. Cover and soak overnight. Place in a large pan and bring to the boil, then reduce the heat and simmer for 5 minutes. Remove the pan from the heat and stir in 1 cup (250 ml/8 fl oz) liqueur muscat. Make sure the temperature is at least 85°C and spoon the fruit mixture and syrup into clean, warm, wide-neck jars. Seal, label and date. Leave for 1 month before using. Store in a cool, dark place for 6 months. Makes about 1.125 litres (36 fl oz)

Clockwise from top left: Peaches in brandy; muscat fruits; preserved figs in brandy; prunes in port; apricots in rum.

PEACHES IN BRANDY

Place 6–8 (1 kg/2 lb) firm ripe slipstone peaches in a large bowl, cover with boiling water and leave for 30 seconds. Remove the peaches using a slotted spoon and refresh in a bowl of icy water. Remove the skins, cut the peaches in half and gently twist and pull apart to remove the stones. Place 1 cup (250 ml/ 8 fl oz) water and $1/2$ cup (125 g/4 oz) sugar in a large pan, and stir over low heat until all the sugar has dissolved. Bring to the boil, add the peach halves and simmer for 2–3 minutes. Remove the peaches with a slotted spoon and place into a 1 litre (32 fl oz) clean, warm jar. Add a split vanilla bean to the syrup and simmer for 5 minutes. Stir in 1 cup (250 ml/ 8 fl oz) brandy, then, making sure the temperature is at least 85°C, pour the syrup over the peaches, placing the vanilla bean inside the jar. Ensure that the fruit is fully covered with the syrup, leaving a very small space at the top of the jar. Seal and label. Leave for 2 weeks before using. Store in a cool, dry place for up to 6 months.
Makes 1 litre (32 fl oz)

QUINCE JELLY

Preparation time: 20 minutes +
  overnight draining
Total cooking time: 1 hour 30 minutes
Makes 1.5 litres (48 fl oz)

**2 kg (4 lb) ripe yellow
  quinces
¼ cup (60 ml/2 fl oz) lemon
  juice
3 cups (750 g/1½ lb) caster
  sugar, warmed
  (see page 5)**

1 Wipe the quinces clean, then cut
into 5 cm (2 inch) pieces, including the
skin and cores. Place the quince pieces
in a large pan with 2 litres (64 fl oz)
water. Bring slowly to the boil, then
reduce the heat and simmer, covered,
for 1 hour, or until tender. Mash any
firmer pieces with a potato masher.
2 Place a jelly bag in a bowl, cover
with boiling water, drain and suspend
the bag over a large heatproof bowl.
3 Ladle the fruit and liquid into the
bag. Do not push the fruit through the
bag or the jelly will become cloudy.
Cover the top of the bag loosely with a
clean tea towel, without touching the
fruit mixture. Allow the mixture to
drip through the bag overnight, or
until there is no liquid dripping
through the cloth.
4 Put two small plates in the freezer.
Discard the pulp and measure the
liquid. Pour the liquid into a large pan
and stir in the lemon juice. Add
1 cup (250 g/8 oz) of the warmed sugar
for each 1 cup (250 ml/8 fl oz) of liquid.
Stir over low heat for 5 minutes, or until
all the sugar has dissolved. Bring to the
boil and boil rapidly for 20–25 minutes,
stirring often. Skim any scum during

cooking with a skimmer or slotted
spoon. Start testing for setting point.
5 Remove from the heat, place a little
jelly onto one of the cold plates and
place in the freezer for 30 seconds.
When setting point is reached, a skin
will form on the surface and the jelly
will wrinkle when pushed with your

finger. Remove any scum.
6 Pour immediately down the sides
of clean, warm jars, and seal. Turn
upside down for 2 minutes, then
invert and leave to cool. Label and
date. Store in a cool, dark place for
6–12 months. Refrigerate after
opening for up to 6 weeks.

*Cut the quinces, including skin and cores,
into 5 cm (2 inch) pieces.*

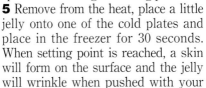

*When the quince is tender, use a potato
masher to break up any firmer pieces.*

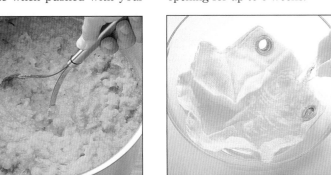

*Pour boiling water over the jelly bag before
suspending it over a heatproof bowl.*

RHUBARB AND GINGER JAM

Preparation time: 15 minutes +
  overnight soaking
Total cooking time: 35 minutes
Makes 1.5 litres (48 fl oz)

**1.5 kg (3 lb) trimmed rhubarb
  (leaves and ends removed)
1.5 kg (3 lb) sugar, warmed
  (see page 5)
1/2 cup (125 ml/4 fl oz) lemon
  juice
4 cm (1 1/2 inch) piece fresh
  ginger, bruised and halved
100 g (3 1/2 oz) glacé ginger**

1 Chop the rhubarb into small pieces. Layer the rhubarb, sugar and lemon juice in a large non-metallic bowl. Cover and leave overnight.
2 Put two small plates in the freezer. Place the rhubarb mixture in a large pan. Finely chop the fresh ginger and place on a square of muslin, tie securely with string and add to the pan. Stir over low heat for 5 minutes, or until all the sugar has dissolved. Bring to the boil and boil rapidly for 20–30 minutes, stirring often. Remove any scum during cooking with a skimmer or slotted spoon. When the jam falls from a tilted wooden spoon in thick sheets without dripping, start testing for setting point.
3 Remove from the heat, place a little

jam onto one of the cold plates and place in the freezer for 30 seconds. When setting point is reached, a skin will form on the surface and the jam will wrinkle when pushed with your finger. Remove any scum and discard the muslin bag. Finely chop the glacé ginger and add to the pan.
4 Spoon immediately into clean, warm jars, and seal. Turn upside down for 2 minutes, then invert and leave to cool. Label and date. Store in a cool, dark place for 6–12 months. Refrigerate after opening for up to 6 weeks.

COOK'S FILE

Note: The amount of ginger can be varied, according to taste.

Discard the leaves and ends from the rhubarb and chop the stalks into pieces.

When the jam has thickened, start testing for setting point.

Remove any scum from the surface and stir in the glacé ginger.

APRICOT JAM

Preparation time: 20 minutes
Total cooking time: 45 minutes
Makes 3 cups (750 ml/24 fl oz)

1 kg (2 lb) apricots, stones removed, quartered
1 kg (2 lb) sugar, warmed (see page 5)

1 Put two small plates in the freezer. Put the apricots in a large pan with 1 1/2 cups (375 ml/12 fl oz) water. Bring to the boil, stirring, for 20 minutes, or until the fruit has softened.

2 Add the sugar and stir, without boiling, for 5 minutes, or until all the sugar has dissolved. Return to the boil and boil for 20 minutes, stirring often. Stir across the base of the pan to check that the jam is not sticking or burning. Remove any scum during cooking with a skimmer or slotted spoon. When the jam falls from a tilted wooden spoon in thick sheets without dripping, start testing for setting point.

3 Remove from the heat, place a little jam onto one of the cold plates and place in the freezer for 30 seconds. When setting point is reached, a skin will form on the surface and the jam will wrinkle when pushed with your finger. Remove any scum.

4 Spoon immediately into clean, warm jars and seal. Turn the jars upside down for 2 minutes, then invert and leave to cool. Label and date. Store in a cool, dark place for 6–12 months. Refrigerate after opening for up to 6 weeks.

Boil the quartered apricots in a large pan for 20 minutes, or until soft.

Start testing for setting point when the jam falls from a spoon without dripping.

A skin will form on the surface of the jam when setting point has been reached.

BANANA JAM

Preparation time: 10 minutes
Total cooking time: 50 minutes
Makes 3 cups (750 ml/24 fl oz)

1 kg (2 lb) very ripe bananas
    (about 7), peeled (see Note)
100 ml (3¹/2 fl oz) lemon juice
3 cups (750 g/1¹/2 lb) sugar,
    warmed (see page 5)

1 Put two small plates in the freezer. Chop the bananas and place in a large pan with the lemon juice and sugar. Bring to the boil and skim any scum with a skimmer or slotted spoon.
2 Cook the jam over medium heat for 30 minutes, then reduce the heat and simmer, stirring frequently, for 15–20 minutes, or until the jam is thick and pale red in colour. Remove any scum from the surface.
3 Spoon immediately into clean, warm jars, and seal. Turn upside down for 2 minutes, then invert and leave to cool. Label and date. Store in a cool, dark place for 6–12 months. Refrigerate after opening for up to 6 weeks.

COOK'S FILE

Note: Use old, mushy bananas, similar to those you would use for a banana cake. While not a true jam, it is just as delicious. Serve as you would other fruit jams.

Use a sharp knife to chop the ripe bananas into small pieces.

Bring the mixture to the boil and skim off any scum that comes to the surface.

Stir often for 15–20 minutes, or until the mixture thickens.

THREE-FRUIT MARMALADE

Preparation time: 30 minutes
  + overnight soaking
Total cooking time: 2 hours 5 minutes
Makes 3.25 litres (104 fl oz)

1 grapefruit
2 oranges
2 lemons
3 kg (6 lb) sugar, warmed
  (see page 5)

1 Scrub the fruit under warm, running water with a soft bristle brush to remove the wax coating. Quarter the grapefruit and halve the oranges and lemons, slice them thinly and place in a non-metallic bowl. Retain the pips and place them on a square of muslin and tie securely with string. Add the muslin bag to the bowl with 2.5 litres (80 fl oz) water, cover and leave overnight.

2 Put two small plates in the freezer. Put the fruit and water in a large pan. Bring to the boil, then reduce the heat and simmer, covered, for 1 hour, or until the fruit is tender.

3 Add the sugar and stir over low heat, without boiling, for 5 minutes, or until all the sugar has dissolved. Return to the boil and boil rapidly for 50–60 minutes, stirring often. Remove any scum during cooking with a skimmer or slotted spoon. When the marmalade falls from a tilted wooden spoon in thick sheets without dripping, start testing for setting point.

4 Remove from the heat, place a little marmalade onto one of the cold plates and place in the freezer for 30 seconds. When setting point is reached, a skin will form on the surface and the marmalade will wrinkle when pushed with your finger. Discard the muslin bag. Remove any scum from the surface.

5 Spoon immediately into clean, warm jars, and seal. Turn upside down for 2 minutes, then invert and leave to cool. Label and date. Store in a cool, dark place for 6–12 months. Refrigerate after opening for up to 6 weeks.

Scrub the fruit under warm, running water with a soft bristle brush.

Cut the prepared fruit into very thin slices before putting in a non-metallic bowl.

When all the fruit is tender, add the warmed sugar to the pan.

SEVILLE ORANGE MARMALADE

Preparation time: 30 minutes +
  overnight soaking
Total cooking time: 1 hour
  30 minutes
Makes 2.5 litres (80 fl oz)

4 Seville oranges
  (about 1.25 kg/2¹/2 lb)
2–2.25 kg (4–4¹/2 lb) sugar,
  warmed (see page 5)

1 Scrub the oranges under warm, running water with a soft bristle brush to remove any wax coating. Cut the oranges in half, and then in half again. Slice the oranges thinly, removing and retaining the pips. Place the pips on a square of muslin and tie securely with a piece of string. Place the orange and muslin bag in a large non-metallic bowl. Cover the fruit and pips with 2 litres (64 fl oz) water and leave overnight.

2 Put two small plates in the freezer. Place the fruit and muslin bag in a large pan. Bring slowly to the boil, then reduce the heat and simmer, covered, for 45 minutes, or until the fruit is tender.

3 Measure the fruit and for every cup (250 ml/8 fl oz) of the fruit mixture add 1 cup (250 g/8 oz) of the warmed sugar. Stir over low heat, without boiling, for 5 minutes, or until all the sugar has dissolved. Return to the boil and boil rapidly for 30–40 minutes, stirring often. Remove any scum during cooking with a skimmer or slotted spoon. When the marmalade falls from a tilted wooden spoon in thick sheets without dripping, start testing for setting point.

4 Remove from the heat, place a little marmalade onto one of the cold plates and place in the freezer for 30 seconds. When setting point is reached, a skin will form on the surface and the marmalade will wrinkle when pushed with your finger. Discard the muslin bag. Remove any scum from the surface.

5 Spoon immediately into clean, warm jars and seal. Turn upside down for 2 minutes, then invert and cool. Label and date. Store in a cool, dark place for 6–12 months. Refrigerate after opening for up to 6 weeks.

COOK'S FILE

Note: Seville oranges are tropical or semi-tropical fruits that make great marmalade due to their thick, rough skin and tart flesh. They are generally only used in cooking.

Cut the oranges in half, then in half again, and slice thinly.

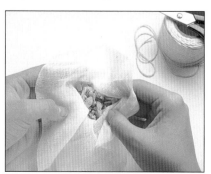

Put the orange pips on a piece of muslin and tie securely with string.

CANDIED FRUIT

Candying fruit takes 8–10 days but it will keep for up to a year if stored between sheets of greaseproof paper in an airtight container in a cool, dry place. Candy types of fruit separately to avoid flavours mixing. Fruits with strong flavours are suitable for candying. These include pineapple, citrus peel, apricots, peaches, pears, figs, plums and cherries. Citrus peel should be cut into quarters or strips. To avoid any bitterness in the pith, blanch the peel in boiling water and refresh in cold water 2–3 times for 5 minutes each time before cooking.

DAY	FRUIT	SUGAR	METHOD	SOAKING/ DRYING TIME
1	500 g (1 lb) fresh fruit	Add 250 g (8 oz) to 1 litre (32 fl oz) water	Dissolve the sugar in the water in a large pan. Add the juice of 1 lemon, and bring to the boil. Add the fruit and poach until just tender but holding its shape (cooking times vary for the fruit used). Place in a heatproof bowl and weigh down with a saucer.	24 hours
	500 g (1 lb) canned fruit in syrup	Drain the fruit, reserving the liquid and make up to 1 litre (32 fl oz) with water. Add 250 g (8 oz) to each litre liquid.	Dissolve the sugar in the water in a large pan. Add the juice of 1 lemon and bring to the boil. Place the fruit in a heatproof bowl and pour over the boiling syrup. Weigh down.	24 hours
2	Fresh/canned	Drain the fruit, add 100 g (3 1/2 oz) to every 1 litre (32 fl oz) liquid	Return the syrup to the pan, add the sugar and stir to dissolve. Bring to the boil and pour over the fruit. Weigh down.	24 hours
3	Fresh/canned	Drain the fruit, add 100 g (3 1/2 oz) to every 1 litre (32 fl oz) liquid	Repeat method as above	24 hours
4	Fresh/canned	Add 150 g (5 oz) per 1 litre (32 fl oz) liquid	Repeat method as above	24 hours
5	Fresh/canned	Add 150 g (5 oz) per 1 litre (32 fl oz) liquid	Repeat method as above	24 hours
6	Fresh/canned	Add 250 g (8 oz) per 1 litre (32 fl oz) liquid	Repeat method as above	24 hours
7	Fresh/canned	No extra sugar added at this step	Put the fruit and syrup in a large pan and bring to the boil, then reduce the heat and simmer for 5 minutes. Drain the fruit on a wire rack over a tray.	24 hours drying time
8	Fresh/canned	Add 500 g (1 lb) to 150 ml (5 fl oz) water for glacé	To glacé the fruit, make up a fresh sugar syrup and boil for 1 minute. Keep hot and cover with a lid to stop evaporation. Pour a little of the hot syrup into a small bowl and dip each piece of drained fruit first in boiling water and then in the syrup, then place on a rack to drain. If the syrup becomes cloudy, start again. Place the fruit on wire racks and put in an oven heated to the lowest temperature, with the door slightly ajar, until dry and no longer sticky.	12 hours– 3 days
		Enough to coat 500 g (1 lb) fruit	To crystallize the fruit, dip each piece of fruit in boiling water, shake off any excess and then roll in caster sugar. Place on wire racks and allow to dry.	

TRADITIONAL FRUIT MINCE

Preparation time: 20 minutes
Total cooking time: nil
Makes 2 litres (64 fl oz)

2 large green apples
    (about 440 g/14 oz), peeled,
    cored and finely chopped
250 g (8 oz) packet suet mix
1¹/₂ cups (345 g/11 oz), firmly
    packed soft brown sugar
375 g (12 oz) raisins

250 g (8 oz) sultanas
250 g (8 oz) currants
150 g (5 oz) mixed peel
100 g (3¹/₂ oz) slivered almonds,
    chopped
1 tablespoon mixed spice
¹/₂ teaspoon nutmeg
¹/₂ teaspoon cinnamon
2 teaspoons grated orange rind
1 teaspoon grated lemon rind
1 cup (250 ml/8 fl oz) orange
    juice
¹/₂ cup (125 ml/4 fl oz) lemon
    juice
150 ml (5 fl oz) brandy

1 Combine all the ingredients and ¹/₂ cup (125 ml/4 fl oz) of the brandy in a large bowl. Mix together thoroughly.
2 Spoon the fruit mince into clean, warm jars. Use a skewer to remove air bubbles and to pack the mixture in firmly. Leave a 1.5 cm (⁵/₈ inch) space at the top of the jar and wipe the jar clean with a cloth. Spoon a little brandy over the surface of the fruit mince and seal. Label and date.
3 Set aside for at least 3 weeks, or up to 6 months, before using in pies and tarts. You should keep the fruit mince refrigerated in hot weather.

Peel and core the apples. Cut them into quarters and then finely chop.

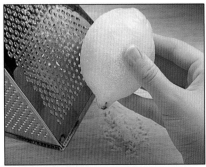

Take care when grating the rind not to include any pith as it will taste bitter.

Remove any air bubbles with a clean metal skewer before sealing the jar.

34

QUICK FRUIT MINCE

Preparation time: 20 minutes
Total cooking time: nil
Makes 2 cups (500 ml/16 fl oz)

1/4 cup (35 g/1 1/4 oz) currants
1/3 cup (40 g/1 1/4 oz) sultanas
2 tablespoons mixed peel
1/4 cup (30 g/1 oz) slivered
 almonds
1 apple, grated

1/4 cup (45 g/1 1/2 oz) soft brown
 sugar
1/4 teaspoon ground nutmeg
1/4 teaspoon ground cinnamon
1 teaspoon grated orange rind
1 teaspoon grated lemon rind
100 g (3 1/2 oz) can stoneless
 cherries, drained and
 quartered, or 150 g (5 oz)
 fresh cherries, pitted
100 g (3 1/2 oz) white seedless
 grapes, halved
1 tablespoon whisky

1 To make the fruit mince mixture, combine all the ingredients in a large bowl and stir well.
2 Spoon into clean, warm jars and seal. Label and date.

COOK'S FILE

Note: Use this quick fruit mince as a filling for mini tarts or as a topping for pancakes. It will only keep for a short period (up to 5 days in the refrigerator) because it is made with fresh fruit and has very little alcohol.

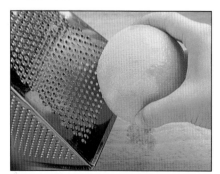

Finely grate the rind—do not grate any white pith as it will taste bitter.

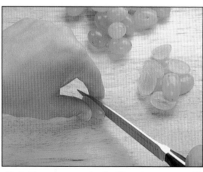

Cut the grapes in half using a small, sharp knife.

Combine all the ingredients in a large bowl and mix well.

FROZEN BERRY JAM

Preparation time: 10 minutes
Total cooking time: 1 hour 15 minutes
Makes 1 litre (32 fl oz)

300 g (10 oz) frozen blackberries
300 g (10 oz) frozen raspberries
300 g (10 oz) frozen blueberries
1/4 cup (60 ml/2 fl oz) lemon
juice, reserving any pips
3 cups (750 g/1 1/2 lb) sugar,
warmed (see page 5)

1 Put two small plates in the freezer. Put the frozen berries in a large pan with 3 cups (750 ml/24 fl oz) water and the lemon juice.

2 Place the pips on a square of muslin and tie securely with string. Add to the pan. Bring to the boil, then reduce the heat and simmer for 30 minutes.

3 Add the sugar and stir over low heat for 5 minutes, or until all the sugar has dissolved. Return to the boil and boil for 30–40 minutes, stirring often. Remove any scum during cooking with a skimmer or slotted spoon. When the jam falls from a tilted wooden spoon in thick sheets without dripping, start testing for setting point.

4 Remove from the heat, place a little jam onto one of the cold plates and place in the freezer for 30 seconds. A skin will form on the surface and the jam will wrinkle when pushed with your finger when setting point is reached. Discard the muslin bag. Remove any scum from the surface.

5 Spoon immediately into clean, warm jars and seal. Turn the jars upside down for 2 minutes, then invert and leave to cool. Label and date. Store in a cool, dark place for 6–12 months. Refrigerate after opening for up to 6 weeks.

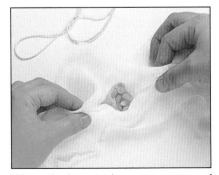

Place the lemon pips on a square of muslin and tie securely with string.

Remove any scum from the surface with a skimmer or slotted spoon.

Setting point is reached when the jam wrinkles when pushed.

PINEAPPLE AND MANGO JAM

Preparation time: 30 minutes
Total cooking time: 45 minutes
Makes 1 litre (32 fl oz)

1 ripe pineapple
2 large mangoes
1 teaspoon lemon rind, grated
1/3 cup (80 ml/2³/4 fl oz) lemon juice, reserving the pips and skin of 1 lemon
1.2 kg (2 lb 6¹/2 oz) warmed sugar (see page 5)

1 Put two small plates in the freezer. Remove the skin and tough eyes from the pineapple. Cut into quarters lengthways, remove the core and cut the flesh into 1 cm (1/2 inch) pieces. Peel the mango and cut each mango cheek from the stone. Cut into 1 cm (1/2 inch) pieces. Place the pineapple, mango, any juices, lemon rind and juice, and sugar in a large pan. Stir for 5 minutes, or until all the sugar has dissolved.
2 Place the reserved pips and skin onto a square of muslin and tie securely with string. Add to the pan.
3 Bring to the boil, then reduce the heat and simmer, stirring often, for 30–40 minutes, or until setting point is reached. Remove any scum during cooking with a skimmer or slotted spoon. Stir across the base of the pan to check that the jam is not sticking or burning. Be careful, the jam will froth. When the jam falls from a tilted wooden spoon in thick sheets without dripping, start testing for setting point.
4 Remove from the heat, place a little jam onto one of the cold plates and place in the freezer for 30 seconds. A skin will form on the surface and the

jam will wrinkle when pushed with your finger when setting point is reached. Remove any scum from the surface.
5 Pour immediately into clean, warm jars and seal. Turn upside down for 2 minutes, then invert and cool. Label and date. Store in a cool, dark place for 6–12 months. Refrigerate after opening for up to 6 weeks.

Remove the skin and any tough eyes from the pineapple.

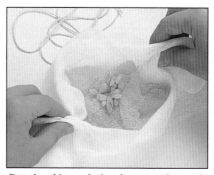

Put the skin and pips from one lemon in a muslin bag and tie with string.

The jam will wrinkle when pushed with your finger when setting point is reached.

GRAPE JELLY

Preparation time: 15 minutes +
  overnight draining
Total cooking time: 1 hour 5 minutes
Makes 2 cups (500 ml/16 fl oz)

2 kg (4 lb) black seedless grapes
1/3 cup (80 ml/2³/4 fl oz)
   lemon juice,
   reserving any pips
2¹/4 cups (560 g/1 lb 2 oz)
   sugar, warmed (see page 5)

1 Remove the stems from the grapes. Place the grapes in a large pan and add 1 cup (250 ml/8 fl oz) water. Place the lemon pips onto a square of muslin and tie securely with string. Add to the pan. Slowly bring to the boil, then reduce the heat and simmer for 30–35 minutes, or until the grapes are soft and pulpy. Remove and discard the muslin bag.
2 Place a jelly bag in a bowl, cover with boiling water, drain and suspend the bag over a large heatproof bowl.
3 Ladle the grape mixture into the jelly bag. Do not push the fruit through the bag or the jelly will become cloudy. Cover the top of the bag loosely with a clean tea towel, without touching the fruit mixture, and allow the mixture to drip through the bag overnight, or until there is no liquid dripping through the cloth.
4 Discard the pulp and measure the liquid. Pour the liquid into a stainless steel or enamel pan and stir in the lemon juice. Add ³/4 cup (185 g/6 oz) sugar for each cup (250 ml/8 fl oz) liquid. Stir over low heat until all the sugar has dissolved, then bring to the boil and boil rapidly, stirring often, for 20–25 minutes, skimming any scum during cooking with a skimmer or slotted spoon.
5 Transfer to a heatproof jug and immediately pour the jelly down the sides of clean, warm jars and seal.

Turn upside down for 2 minutes, then invert and leave to cool. Label and date. Store in a cool, dark place for 6–12 months. Refrigerate after opening for up to 6 weeks.

Suspend the jelly bag over a large heatproof bowl and let the mixture drip through.

When there is no more liquid dripping through the cloth, discard the pulp.

Gently pour the jelly down the sides of clean, warm jars and seal.

Halve each cumquat, removing and retaining the pips.

Pour the cumquats, muslin bag and lemon juice into a large pan.

Boil the marmalade, without stirring, for 20 minutes, then test for setting point.

CUMQUAT MARMALADE

Preparation time: 20 minutes +
 overnight soaking
Total cooking time: 1 hour
Makes 1.75 litres (56 fl oz)

1 kg (2 lb) cumquats
¼ cup (60 ml/2 fl oz) lemon juice
1.25 kg (2½ lb) sugar, warmed
 (see page 5)

1 Scrub the cumquats under warm, running water with a soft bristle brush to remove the wax coating. Remove and discard the stems. Halve each lengthways, removing and retaining the pips, and slice finely. Place the pips onto a square of muslin and tie securely with string. Put the fruit and pips in a large non-metallic bowl. Add 1.25 litres (40 fl oz) water, cover with plastic wrap and leave overnight.
2 Put two small plates in the freezer. Place the cumquats and muslin bag in

a large pan with the lemon juice. Bring slowly to the boil, then reduce the heat and simmer, covered, for 30 minutes, or until the fruit is tender.
3 Add the warmed sugar. Stir over low heat, without boiling, for 5 minutes, or until all the sugar has dissolved. Return the mixture to the boil and boil rapidly, stirring frequently, for 20 minutes. Skim any scum from the surface during cooking with a skimmer or slotted spoon. When the marmalade falls from a tilted wooden spoon in thick sheets without dripping, start testing for setting point.
4 Remove the pan from the heat, place a little marmalade onto one of the cold plates and place in the freezer for 30 seconds. A skin will form on the surface and the marmalade will wrinkle when pushed with your finger when setting point is reached. Discard the muslin bag. Remove any scum from the surface.
5 Spoon immediately into clean, warm jars. Turn upside down for

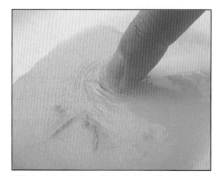

The marmalade will wrinkle when pushed when setting point is reached.

2 minutes, then invert and leave to cool. Label and date. Store in a cool, dark place for 6–12 months. Refrigerate after opening for up to 6 weeks.

DRIED FRUITS

Dried fruits make a simple, yet delicious, snack for children to nibble on instead of crisps or lollies. You can also use crisp dried fruits, lightly dusted with icing sugar, as an eye-catching garnish on a fruit mousse. The drying process results in an intense, concentrated fruit flavour sure to delight both young and old. Almost any fruits can be successfully dried, except berries and those with a high water content. It is very important to keep dried fruits cool and dry, otherwise they will discolour or go mouldy. Dried fruit can be kept in an airtight container in a cool, dry place for up to 2 weeks.

Before you start the drying process, think about how you are going to slice the fruit to make it look its best. Apples, for example, are best sliced across the middle, while pears are best sliced lengthways. Fruit such as rhubarb can be shaped during the cooling process.

A mandolin is a hand-held slicer with extremely sharp, adjustable blades. Always use the safety shield when slicing. If you have one, a mandolin will make slicing some of the smaller fruit much easier. If you don't have a mandolin, you just need a good, sharp knife, so be careful!

You can pick the fruit you wish to dry because of its shape, for example, star fruit. Adding lemon juice helps the fruit keep its colour, as does the sugar, but check your fruit regularly while it is drying to make sure it doesn't burn or get too brown. Cool any fruit thoroughly before storing it in an airtight container—it should keep for a few days before softening but can be quickly refreshed in the oven until it dries out again.

PINEAPPLE

Peel and remove the tough eyes from a medium-sized pineapple, then cut the flesh into 2 mm (1/8 inch) slices. Pat the slices dry with paper towels and spread them out on baking trays lined with baking paper. Sprinkle the pineapple slices lightly with sugar and cook in an oven at the lowest possible temperature for 3 hours. Turn the slices over approximately halfway through the cooking process. Check every now and then to make sure the pineapple pieces don't get too dark or burn. Remove the pineapple carefully from the baking trays when dry and cool completely before storing in an airtight container.

APPLES AND PEARS

Slice 2 apples and 2 pears as thinly as you can, about 2 mm (1/8 inch) thick, if possible, leaving the skin and core intact. Cut the apples through the middle to get a pretty star-shaped pattern from the core. Cut the pears through their length. Put both the apple and pear slices in a bowl, sprinkle them with a little lemon juice and toss to coat thoroughly. Pat the fruit slices dry with paper towels and spread out on baking trays lined with baking paper. Sprinkle the apple and pear slices lightly with sugar and cook in an oven at the lowest possible temperature for 2 1/2–3 hours. Turn the slices over approximately halfway through the cooking process. Check every now and then to make sure the fruit pieces don't get too dark or burn. Remove the apple and pear slices carefully from the tray when dry and cool completely before storing in an airtight container.

STAR FRUIT

Cut 2 or 3 star fruit into 2 mm (1/8 inch) slices and sprinkle with the juice of half a lemon. Pat the star fruit slices dry with paper towels and spread out on baking trays lined with baking paper. Sprinkle lightly with sugar and cook in an oven at the lowest possible temperature for 2–2 1/2 hours. Turn the slices over approximately halfway through the cooking process. Check every now and then to make sure they don't get too dark or burn. Remove the star fruit carefully from the tray when dry and cool completely before storing in an airtight container.

RHUBARB

Remove the string and trim the ends from 2 or 3 rhubarb stems and slice into long, thin strips along the length of the fruit. Pat the rhubarb slices dry with paper towels and spread out on baking trays lined with baking paper. Sprinkle lightly with sugar. Cook in an oven at the lowest possible temperature for 2 1/2–3 hours. Turn the slices over approximately halfway through the cooking process. Check every now and then to make sure the rhubarb pieces don't get too dark or burn. Remove the rhubarb carefully from the tray when dry and then cool completely before storing in an airtight container. If you want to be a little more creative, you can try wrapping the cooked rhubarb around the handle of a wooden spoon when cooling.

Note: To keep the fruit as crisp as possible, spread a thin layer of uncooked rice on the base of an airtight container, cover with baking paper and top with the fruit. The rice will absorb any excess moisture.

Drying times may vary greatly, depending on the fruit chosen, the season and oven temperatures.

Clockwise from top left: Pineapple; pear; star fruit; rhubarb; apple.

BLACKBERRY AND APPLE JAM

Preparation time: 20 minutes
Total cooking time: 55 minutes
Makes 1.75 litres (56 fl oz)

750 g (1¹/2 lb) green apples
1 kg (2 lb) blackberries
1.5 kg (3 lb) sugar, warmed
  (see page 5)

1 Put two small plates in the freezer. Peel, core and chop the apples. Place the apple pieces in a large pan with the berries and ¹/2 cup (125 ml/4 fl oz) water. Cook, covered, over medium heat, stirring often, for 30 minutes, or until the fruit has softened.
2 Add the sugar and stir, without boiling, for 5 minutes, or until all the sugar has dissolved.
3 Bring the jam to the boil and boil for 20 minutes, stirring often. Stir across the base of the pan to check that the jam is not sticking or burning. When the jam falls from a tilted wooden spoon in thick sheets without dripping, start testing for setting point.

4 Remove from the heat, place a little jam onto one of the cold plates and place in the freezer for 30 seconds. A skin will form on the surface and the jam will wrinkle when pushed with your finger when setting point is reached. Remove any scum from the surface with a skimmer or slotted spoon.
5 Transfer to a heatproof jug and immediately pour into clean, warm jars, and seal. Turn upside down for 2 minutes, then invert and leave to cool. Label and date. Store in a cool, dark place for 6–12 months. Refrigerate after opening for up to 6 weeks.

Test for setting point when the jam falls from a tilted wooden spoon in thick sheets.

The jam will wrinkle when pushed with your finger when setting point is reached.

Transfer the jam to a heatproof jug before pouring into clean, warm jars.

MELON AND LEMON CONSERVE

Preparation time: 25 minutes
Total cooking time: 1 hour 45 minutes
Makes 1 litre (32 fl oz)

2.5 kg (5 lb) honeydew melons
6 lemons
1 tablespoon brandy
1.25 kg (2½ lb) sugar, warmed
(see page 5)

1 Put two small plates in the freezer. Peel and seed the melons. Cut into 1 cm (½ inch) cubes and add to a large pan.
2 Scrub the lemons under hot, running water with a soft bristle brush to remove the wax coating, then cut them in half. Juice the lemons, retaining the pips, and add the juice to the pan. Roughly chop the lemons and divide the pieces and the pips between two squares of muslin. Tie securely with string and add to the pan along with the brandy and 3 cups (750 ml/24 fl oz) water. Bring to the boil and boil for 40 minutes, or until the fruit is soft.
3 Add the sugar and stir over low heat, without boiling, for 5 minutes, or until all the sugar has dissolved. Bring to the boil and boil, stirring often, for 30 minutes. As the mixture thickens and starts to darken, reduce the heat and simmer, stirring frequently, for 20–30 minutes. When the conserve falls from a tilted wooden spoon in thick sheets without dripping, start testing for setting point.
4 Remove from the heat, place a little conserve onto one of the cold plates and place in the freezer for 30 seconds. A skin will form on the surface and the conserve will wrinkle when pushed with your finger when setting point is reached. Discard the muslin bags. Remove any scum from the surface.
5 Spoon immediately into clean, warm jars and seal. Turn upside down for 2 minutes, then invert and leave to cool. Label and date. Store in a cool, dark place for 6–12 months. Refrigerate after opening for up to 6 weeks.

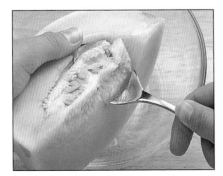

Scoop out the seeds of the melons and then cut off the skin.

Roughly chop the lemons after squeezing the juice from them.

When the fruit is soft and tender, add all the warmed sugar to the pan.

43

POMEGRANATE JELLY

Preparation time: 15 minutes +
  overnight draining
Total cooking time: 50 minutes
Makes 2 cups (500 ml/16 fl oz)

**2–2.5 kg (4–5 lb) pomegranates
  (about 8 pomegranates)
3 green apples
about 2 cups (500 g/1 lb)
  caster sugar, warmed
  (see page 5)
1/4 cup (60 ml/2 fl oz) lemon juice**

1 Cut the pomegranates in half and use a juicer to squeeze the juice out of them. At least 2 cups (500 ml/16 fl oz) of pomegranate juice will be needed.

2 Chop the apples, including the skin and cores. Place in a large pan with the pomegranate juice and 1 cup (250 ml/8 fl oz) water. Bring slowly to the boil, then reduce the heat and simmer, covered, for 20 minutes, or until the apple is mushy.

3 Place a jelly bag in a large bowl, cover with boiling water, drain and suspend the bag over a large heatproof bowl. Alternatively, scald a large square of cheesecloth or a clean tea towel and suspend the fabric between the legs of an upturned stool by tying the corners with string, leaving the fabric loose enough to form a slight dip in the centre. Place a large heatproof bowl under the cloth.

4 Ladle the fruit and liquid into the bag. Do not push the fruit through the bag or the jelly will become cloudy. Cover the top of the bag loosely with a clean tea towel, without touching the fruit mixture. Allow the mixture to drip through the bag overnight, or until there is no liquid dripping through the cloth.

5 Put two small plates in the freezer. Discard the pulp and measure the liquid. Pour the liquid into a large pan. Add the sugar—1 cup (250 g/8 oz) for every cup (250 ml/8 fl oz) of the liquid—and stir over medium heat until all the sugar has dissolved. Stir in the lemon juice. Bring to the boil and boil rapidly for 15–20 minutes, stirring often. Skim any scum off the surface with a skimmer or slotted spoon during cooking. Start testing for setting point.

6 Remove from the heat, place a little jelly onto one of the cold plates and place in the freezer for 30 seconds. A skin will form on the surface and the jelly will wrinkle when pushed with your finger when setting point is reached. Remove any scum from the surface.

7 Stand the clean, warm jars on a wooden board or a cloth-covered surface. Carefully transfer the jelly to a heatproof jug. Wrap the jars in a cloth to protect your hands. Tilt the jar and pour the jelly down the sides of the jars to stop bubbles forming. Seal the jars while hot and gently turn upside down for 2 minutes, then invert and leave to cool. Label and date. Store in a cool, dark place for 6–12 months. Refrigerate after opening for up to 6 weeks.

COOK'S FILE

Note: The amount of juice in the fruit varies and consequently the amount of sugar required will also vary.
Pomegranates are rich in vitamin C and high in fibre. The juice is boiled down with sugar to create a thick, sweet syrup called grenadine, which is used in drinks and sweet dishes.

Cut the pomegranates in half and squeeze the juice out of them.

Ladle the fruit and liquid into the jelly bag and leave overnight to drain.

Stir the lemon juice in and boil the mixture for 15–20 minutes.

Skim off any scum that forms on the surface with a skimmer or slotted spoon.

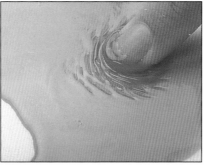
When setting point is reached, the jelly will wrinkle when you push it.

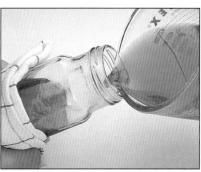
Transfer the jelly to a jug and gently pour into the jars.

45

BLACK CHERRY JAM

Preparation time: 30 minutes
Total cooking time: 1 hour
Makes 3 cups (750 ml/24 fl oz)

1 kg (2 lb) fresh black cherries
½ cup (125 ml/4 fl oz)
lemon juice
3 cups (750 g/1½ lb) sugar,
warmed (see page 5)
25 g (¾ oz) jam-setting
mixture, if required

1 Put two small plates in the freezer. Remove the stalks from the cherries and, using a small sharp knife, cut the cherries open and remove the pips. Alternatively, use a cherry pitter, available from kitchenware stores. Place the pips onto a square piece of muslin and tie securely with string.

2 Place the cherries and muslin bag in a large pan together with 1 cup (250 ml/8 fl oz) water and the lemon juice. Bring to the boil, then reduce the heat and simmer, stirring often, for 30 minutes, or until the cherries are tender. Discard the muslin bag.

3 Add the sugar and stir over low heat, without boiling, for 5 minutes, or until all the sugar has dissolved. Return to the boil and boil for 15–20 minutes, stirring often. Remove any scum with a skimmer or slotted spoon.

4 Remove from the heat, place a little jam onto one of the cold plates and place in the freezer for 30 seconds. A skin will form on the surface and the jam will wrinkle when pushed with your finger when setting point is reached. If the jam doesn't set, add the jam-setting mixture, return to the heat and boil rapidly for 5 minutes. Remove any scum from the surface.

5 Spoon immediately into clean, warm jars and seal. Turn the jars upside down for 2 minutes, then invert and leave to cool. Label and date. Store in a cool, dark place for 6–12 months. Refrigerate after opening for up to 6 weeks.

COOK'S FILE

Note: Cherries are low in pectin and jam-setting mixture is often added. If it is unavailable, boil the jam for a little longer and add more lemon juice.

Place the cherry pips onto a square of muslin and tie securely with string.

Add the warmed sugar to the mixture and stir, without boiling, for 5 minutes.

Carefully remove any scum from the surface with a skimmer or a slotted spoon.

SPICED DRIED PEACH CONSERVE

Preparation time: 15 minutes +
  overnight soaking
Total cooking time: 50 minutes
Makes 1.25 litres (40 fl oz)

**400 g (13 oz) dried peaches,
  cut into 2 or 3 pieces
2 cinnamon sticks
3 cloves
3 cardamom pods
1.25 kg (2¹/2 lb) sugar, warmed
  (see page 5)
¹/4 cup (60 ml/2 fl oz) lemon
  juice**

1 Place the dried peaches in a non-metallic bowl, add 1.75 litres (56 fl oz) water, cover and soak overnight.
2 Put two small plates in the freezer. Pour the peaches and water into a large pan. Place the spices on a square of muslin and tie securely with string. Add to the pan with 1 cup (250 ml/ 8 fl oz) water. Bring to the boil, then reduce the heat and simmer for 20 minutes, or until the fruit is soft.
3 Add the sugar and lemon juice and stir over low heat, without boiling, for 5 minutes, or until all the sugar has dissolved. Return to the boil and boil for 20–25 minutes, stirring often. Remove any scum from the surface during cooking with a skimmer or

slotted spoon. When the conserve falls from a tilted wooden spoon in thick sheets without dripping, start testing for setting point.
4 Remove from the heat, place a little conserve onto one of the cold plates and place in the freezer for 30 seconds. A skin will form on the surface and the conserve will wrinkle when pushed with your finger when setting point is reached. Discard the muslin bag. Remove any scum from the surface.
5 Spoon immediately into clean, warm jars. Turn upside down for 2 minutes, then invert and leave to cool. Label and date. Store in a cool, dark place for 6–12 months. Refrigerate after opening for up to 6 weeks.

Cut the dried peaches into two or three pieces using a knife or kitchen scissors.

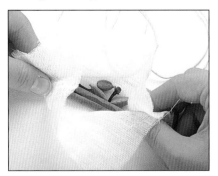

Wrap the spices in a piece of muslin, pull up into a bag and tie securely with string.

When setting point is reached, the conserve will wrinkle when pushed.

CURDS

Fruit curds are delicious spread on toast, scones, croissants or pikelets. They can also be used as fillings for sponge cakes, crêpes, tarts or meringues. If presented in decorated jars, they always make popular gifts, or pour into small jars, label, date and sell at your next school fête. The mixture of fruit and butter gives a rich, creamy consistency and taste which is hard to resist. They will keep for up to two months in the refrigerator—if they last that long!

LEMON CURD

Combine 1 1/2 tablespoons finely grated lemon rind, 3/4 cup (185 ml/6 fl oz) lemon juice, 185 g (6 oz) soft unsalted butter and 1 cup (250 g/8 oz) caster sugar in a heatproof bowl. Place the bowl over a pan of gently simmering water, without touching the water, and stir the mixture until the butter has melted and all the sugar has dissolved. Add 12 egg yolks and stir constantly until the mixture thickens and coats the back of a spoon. This will take about 15–20 minutes—the heat must remain low or the mixture will curdle. Strain the mixture, reheat and then pour into clean, warm jars. Seal while hot, label and date. Keep in the refrigerator for up to 2 months.
Makes about 2 1/2 cups (600 ml/20 fl oz)

MANGO AND LIME CURD

Cut the cheeks from 2 large mangoes, cutting on either side of the stone, peel and chop the flesh. Blend the flesh in a food processor or blender until smooth. Push through a fine sieve—you will need 1 1/4 cups (315 ml/10 fl oz) strained mango purée. Combine the purée with 1/2 teaspoon finely grated lime rind, 1/3 cup (80 ml/2 3/4 fl oz) strained lime juice, 160 g (5 1/2 oz) soft unsalted butter, 1 cup (250 g/8 oz) sugar and 4 beaten eggs in a heat-proof bowl. Place the bowl over a pan of simmering water, without touching the water. Stir constantly until the butter has melted and the sugar has dissolved. Stir for 15–20 minutes, or until the mixture thickens and coats the back of a spoon. Remove from the heat, pour into clean, warm jars and seal while hot. While fresh mango has a better flavour, puréed frozen mango can also be used successfully. Keep in the refrigerator for up to 2 months.
Makes about 3 1/2 cups (875 ml/28 fl oz)

PASSIONFRUIT CURD

Beat 4 eggs and strain into a heat-proof bowl. Stir in 3/4 cup (185 g/6 oz) caster sugar, 3 teaspoons finely grated lemon rind, 1/3 cup (80 ml/2 3/4 fl oz) lemon juice, 1/2 cup (125 g/ 4 oz) passionfruit pulp and 200 g (6 1/2 oz) soft unsalted butter. Place the bowl over a pan of simmering water, without touching the water, and stir until the butter has melted and all the sugar dissolved. Stir constantly for about 15–20 minutes, or until the mixture thickly coats the back of the spoon. Spoon into clean, warm jars and seal while hot. Refrigerate when cool. Keep in the refrigerator for up to 2 months.
Makes 2 1/2 cups (600 ml/20 fl oz)

VANILLA BEAN AND LEMON CURD

Place 2 teaspoons grated lemon rind, 1/2 cup (125 ml/4 fl oz) lemon juice, 125 g (4 oz) soft unsalted butter and 3/4 cup (185 g/6 oz) vanilla-infused caster sugar (see Note) in a pan. Stir over low heat until all the sugar has dissolved. Lightly beat 4 egg yolks and slowly drizzle into the lemon mixture while stirring. Return the mixture to the heat and cook over low heat, stirring constantly, for about 5 minutes, or until thickened. Pour into clean, warm jars and seal while hot. Keep in the refrigerator for up to 2 months.
Makes 1 1/2 cups (375 ml/12 fl oz)

Note: To make vanilla sugar, store a whole vanilla bean with the caster sugar in an airtight container for at least 1 week prior to use. Remove the vanilla bean before use. If washed and dried thoroughly, and stored in an airtight container, the vanilla bean can be reused three or four times.

STRAWBERRY CURD

Hull 250 g (8 oz) strawberries, chop roughly and place in a pan with 3/4 cup (185 g/6 oz) caster sugar, 125 g (4 oz) soft unsalted butter, 1 teaspoon grated lemon rind and 1 tablespoon lemon juice. Stir over low heat until the butter has melted and the sugar dissolved. Simmer gently for 5 minutes, then remove from the heat. Lightly beat 4 egg yolks in a large bowl, then slowly drizzle into the strawberry mixture while stirring. The mixture will thicken as you add it. Return to low heat and cook for 2 minutes while stirring. Do not allow to boil or the curd will separate. Pour into clean, warm jars and seal while hot. Keep in the refrigerator for up to 2 months.
Makes 2 cups (500 ml/16 fl oz)

DRIED APRICOT CURD

Place 100 g (3 1/2 oz) finely chopped dried apricots in a bowl, cover with 1/2 cup (125 ml/4 fl oz) boiling water, and stand for 30 minutes. Stir to form a lumpy paste. Beat 4 eggs well and strain into a heatproof bowl, stir in 1/2 cup (125 g/4 oz) caster sugar, 1/2 cup (125 ml/4 fl oz) lemon juice, 180 g (6 oz) soft unsalted butter and the apricot paste. Place the bowl over a pan of simmering water, without touching the water. Stir until the butter has melted and the sugar dissolved. Stir constantly for about 15–20 minutes, or until the mixture thickly coats the back of a spoon. Spoon into clean, warm jars and seal while hot. Keep in the refrigerator for up to 2 months.
Makes 2 1/2 cups (600 ml/20 fl oz)

Clockwise from top left: Passionfruit curd; dried apricot curd; strawberry curd; lemon curd; mango and lime curd; vanilla bean and lemon curd.

COINTREAU ORANGE MARMALADE

Preparation time: 25 minutes +
  overnight soaking
Total cooking time: 2 hours
Makes 2 litres (64 fl oz)

1 kg (2 lb) oranges
2 kg (4 lb) sugar, warmed
  (see page 5)
1/3 cup (80 ml/2³/₄ fl oz)
  Cointreau

1 Scrub the oranges with a soft bristle brush under warm, running water to remove the wax coating. Cut them in half, then into thin slices, reserving the pips. Place the pips on a square of muslin and tie securely with string. Place the orange slices and muslin bag in a large non-metallic bowl with 2 litres (64 fl oz) water, cover and leave overnight.

2 Put two small plates in the freezer. Transfer the fruit, water and muslin bag to a large pan. Bring slowly to the boil, then reduce the heat and simmer, covered, for 1 hour, or until the fruit is tender and the mixture has reduced by a third.

3 Measure the fruit and for every 1 cup (250 ml/8 fl oz) of the fruit mixture add 1 cup (250 g/8 oz) of the warmed sugar. Stir over low heat, without boiling, for 5 minutes, or until all the sugar has dissolved. Bring to the boil and boil rapidly for 40–50 minutes, stirring often. Remove any scum during cooking with a skimmer or slotted spoon. When the marmalade falls from a tilted wooden spoon in thick sheets without dripping, start testing for setting point.

4 Remove from the heat, place a little

marmalade onto one of the cold plates and place in the freezer for 30 seconds. A skin will form on the surface and the marmalade will wrinkle when pushed with your finger when setting point is reached. Discard the muslin bag. Remove any scum from the

surface. Stir in the Cointreau.

5 Spoon immediately into clean, warm jars. Turn upside down for 2 minutes, then invert and leave to cool. Label and date. Store in a cool, dark place for 6–12 months. Refrigerate after opening for up to 6 weeks.

Cut the scrubbed oranges into halves, then cut into very thin slices.

Simmer the fruit until it is tender and the mixture has reduced by a third.

Remove any scum that has formed on the surface, then stir in the Cointreau.

BOYSENBERRY JAM

Preparation time: 20 minutes
Total cooking time: 35 minutes
Makes 1.25 litres (40 fl oz)

1 kg (2 lb) fresh boysenberries
1/3 cup (80 ml/2³/4 fl oz)
   lemon juice
1 kg (2 lb) sugar, warmed
   (see page 5)

1 Put two small plates in the freezer. Put the berries and lemon juice in a large pan and cook gently for 10 minutes. Add the sugar and stir over low heat for 5 minutes, or until all the sugar has dissolved.

2 Bring to the boil and boil, stirring, for 20 minutes. Remove any scum with a skimmer or slotted spoon during cooking. When the jam falls from a tilted wooden spoon in thick sheets without dripping, start testing for setting point.

3 Remove from the heat, place a little jam onto one of the cold plates and place in the freezer for 30 seconds. A skin will form on the surface and the jam will wrinkle when pushed with your finger when setting point is reached. Remove any scum from the surface.

4 Pour immediately into clean, warm jars and seal. Turn the jars upside down for 2 minutes, then invert and leave to cool. Label and date. Store in a cool, dark place for 6–12 months. Refrigerate after opening for up to 6 weeks.

COOK'S FILE

Note: If boysenberries are not available, any soft berry can be used, such as mulberries, raspberries, or blackberries.

Place the fresh boysenberries in a stainless steel or enamel pan.

The surface of the jam will wrinkle when setting point is reached.

Turn the jars upside down for 2 minutes, then invert and leave to cool.

PEAR AND GINGER CONSERVE

Preparation time: 30 minutes
Total cooking time: 1 hour
Makes 1.5 litres (48 fl oz)

1.5 kg (3 lb) buerre bosc pears
¼ cup (60 ml/2 fl oz) lemon
   juice
1 teaspoon grated lemon rind
1.5 kg (3 lb) sugar, warmed
   (see page 5)
150 g (5 oz) glacé ginger,
   finely chopped

1 Put two small plates in the freezer. Peel, halve and core the pears. Cut the flesh into 1.5 cm (5/8 inch) pieces. Place the cores and seeds on a piece of muslin, gather up and tie securely with string. Add to a large pan with the fruit, lemon juice and rind, and 1 cup (250 ml/8 fl oz) water.
2 Bring to the boil, then reduce the heat and simmer for 20–25 minutes, or until the pear is soft. Add the sugar and glacé ginger and stir over low heat, without boiling, for 5–10 minutes, or until the sugar has dissolved. Return to the boil and boil for 20–25 minutes, stirring often. Remove any scum during cooking with a skimmer or slotted spoon. When the conserve falls from a tilted wooden spoon in thick sheets without dripping, start testing for setting point.
3 Remove from the heat, place a little conserve onto one of the cold plates and place in the freezer for 30 seconds. A skin will form on the surface and the conserve will wrinkle when pushed with your finger when setting point is reached. Discard the muslin bag. Remove any scum from the surface.

4 Spoon immediately into clean, warm jars. Turn upside down for 2 minutes, then invert and leave to cool. Label and date. Store in a cool, dark place for 6–12 months. Refrigerate after opening for up to 6 weeks.

Peel, halve and core the pears and cut the flesh into small pieces.

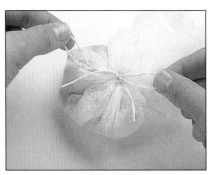

Put the cores and seeds on a piece of muslin and tie into a bag with string.

When the pear is soft, add the glacé ginger and warmed sugar to the pan.

LIME MARMALADE

Preparation time: 20 minutes +
  overnight soaking
Total cooking time: 1 hour 10 minutes
Makes 2.25 litres (72 fl oz)

1 kg (2 lb) limes
2.25 kg (4¹/₂ lb) sugar, warmed
  (see page 5)

1 Scrub the limes under warm, running water with a soft bristle brush to remove the wax coating. Cut in half lengthways, reserving any pips, slice thinly and place in a large non-metallic bowl with 2 litres (64 fl oz) water. Tie any lime pips securely in a square of muslin and add to the bowl. Cover and leave overnight.

2 Put two small plates in the freezer. Place the fruit and water in a large pan. Bring slowly to the boil, then reduce the heat and simmer, covered, for 45 minutes, or until the fruit is tender. Add the sugar and stir over low heat, without boiling, for 5 minutes, or until all the sugar has dissolved. Return to the boil and boil rapidly, stirring often, for 20 minutes. Remove any scum during cooking with a skimmer or slotted spoon. When the marmalade falls from a tilted wooden spoon in thick sheets without dripping, start testing for setting point.

3 Remove from the heat, place a little marmalade onto one of the cold plates and place in the freezer for 30 seconds. A skin will form on the surface and the marmalade will wrinkle when pushed with your finger when setting point is reached. Discard the muslin bag. Remove any scum from the surface.

4 Spoon immediately into clean, warm jars. Turn upside down for 2 minutes, then invert and leave to cool. Label and date. Store in a cool, dark place for 6–12 months. Refrigerate after opening for up to 6 weeks.

COOK'S FILE

Note: Look for brightly coloured limes that feel heavy for their size.

Scrub the limes with a soft bristle brush under warm, running water.

Stir the mixture over low heat, without boiling, until the sugar has dissolved.

Test a little marmalade on a plate to see if setting point has been reached.

WINTER FRUIT CONSERVE

Preparation time: 30 minutes +
  overnight soaking
Total cooking time: 1 hour 30 minutes
Makes 2 litres (64 fl oz)

1.5 kg (3 lb) firm pears,
  peeled and cored
1 grapefruit
1 orange
1 lemon
1.5 kg (3 lb) sugar, warmed
  (see page 5)
2 cups (250 g/8 oz) raisins
1/2 cup (60 g/2 oz) sultanas
1/3 cup (80 ml/2³/4 fl oz) whisky

1 Put the pears in a food processor. Scrub the grapefruit, orange and lemon under warm, running water with a soft bristle brush to remove the wax coating, then halve and thinly slice, removing the pips. Chop the flesh and add to the food processor with any juices. Process in batches until finely chopped and pulpy. Transfer to a large non-metallic bowl. Stir in the sugar, cover and leave overnight.

2 Place the mixture in a large pan and bring to the boil. Reduce the heat and simmer for 45 minutes, stirring often. Remove any scum during cooking with a skimmer or slotted spoon.

3 Add the raisins and sultanas and cook, stirring often, for 45 minutes, or until thick and pulpy. Remove from the heat and stir in the whisky.

4 Spoon immediately into clean, warm jars and seal. Turn upside down for 2 minutes, then invert and leave to cool. Label and date. Store in a cool, dark place for 6–12 months. Refrigerate after opening for up to 6 weeks.

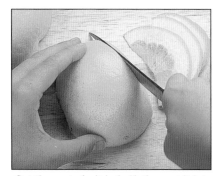

Cut the grapefruit in half, then cut it into very thin slices, removing any pips.

Process the fruit with any juice until it is finely chopped and pulpy.

Add the raisins and sultanas and cook until the conserve is thick and pulpy.

GRAPEFRUIT MARMALADE

Preparation time: 30 minutes +
  overnight soaking
Total cooking time: 1 hour 40 minutes
Makes 2 litres (64 fl oz)

1.25 kg (2½ lb) grapefruit
  (about 3 large)
2 lemons
2.5 kg (5 lb) sugar, warmed
  (see page 5)

1 Scrub the fruit under warm, running water with a soft bristle brush to remove the wax coating. Remove the rind from the fruit in long strips, avoiding the bitter white pith. Cut the strips into 5 cm (2 inch) lengths, then slice thinly. Remove the white pith from the fruit, then chop the flesh, discarding the pips. Place all the fruit and rind in a large non-metallic bowl with 2.5 litres (80 fl oz) water, cover and leave overnight.

2 Put two small plates in the freezer. Place the fruit and water in a large pan, bring to the boil, then reduce the heat and simmer, covered, for 45 minutes, or until the fruit is tender.

3 Add the sugar and stir over low heat, without boiling, for 5 minutes, or until all the sugar has dissolved. Return to the boil and boil, stirring often, for 40–50 minutes, checking frequently in the last 20 minutes. Remove any scum during cooking with a skimmer or slotted spoon. When the marmalade falls from a tilted wooden spoon in thick sheets without dripping, start testing for setting point.

4 Remove from the heat, place a little marmalade onto one of the cold plates and place in the freezer for 30 seconds. A skin will form on the surface and the marmalade will wrinkle when pushed with your finger when setting point is reached. Remove any scum from the surface with a skimmer or slotted spoon.

5 Spoon immediately into clean, warm jars and seal. Turn upside down for 2 minutes, then invert and leave to cool. Label and date. Store in a cool, dark place for 6–12 months. Refrigerate after opening for up to 6 weeks.

Cut the grapefruit and lemon rind into thin strips.

Remove all the white pith from the flesh of the grapefruit.

If using a sugar thermometer, the setting temperature should be about 104°C.

HEAT PROCESSING

Make the most of the abundance of fruit in their peak season and preserve them to be enjoyed up to a year later. Once opened, they will keep for up to a week in the refrigerator.

Use either bottling jars with glass lids, spring clips and rubber seals, or Kilner bottles with metal lids and rubber seals. Ensure the bottles fit snugly into the pot and will be fully submerged in the simmering water.

Ten steps to heat processing

1 Choose just ripe or slightly underripe fruit, without blemishes.
2 Thoroughly wash and dry the bottles.
3 Pack the fruit tightly to allow for shrinkage during processing.
4 Dip the rubber seals into boiling water before placing onto the bottles.
5 To make the sugar syrup, place the sugar and water in a pan. Stir over low heat until dissolved. Brush the sides of the pan with a wet pastry brush to remove any undissolved sugar. Bring to the boil, and boil for 3 minutes.
6 Cover the fruit with hot syrup (85°C). Tap the bottles while filling to remove any air bubbles.
7 Carefully close the lids.
8 Put a folded tea towel on the base of the stockpot. Fill the pot with warm water (38°C) to submerge the bottles.
9 Gradually bring the water to simmering (88–90°C), this may take 25–30 minutes, then simmer steadily for the processing time. Do not allow the water to boil. Check the water level regularly and top up with boiling water, if required.
10 When processing is complete, remove the pot from the heat and remove some water. Wear rubber gloves or use tongs to remove the

bottles. Do not put any pressure on the lids. Place on a wooden board and cool overnight. Label and date.

To test that the seals on the spring-clip bottles are secure, release the clip and, with your fingertips, grip the rim of the lid and carefully lift the bottles. The seals will hold their own weight if properly processed. If they do not, store in the refrigerator and consume within 2 days.

PEARS

Mix 1 litre (32 fl oz) water with 1 teaspoon salt and 1 tablespoon lemon juice, or 1/2 teaspoon citric acid, in a large bowl. Peel 2.75 kg (5 1/2 lb) Beurre Bosc pears, halve and remove the cores. Place each pear in the lemon water mixture. Make a sugar syrup by dissolving 3 cups (750 g/1 1/2 lb) sugar in 1.5 litres (48 fl oz) boiling water and 1/4 cup (60 ml/2 fl oz) lemon juice, or 1 1/2 teaspoons citric acid. Arrange the fruit in six 500 ml (16 fl oz) bottles. Follow the 10 steps to heat processing. Cook for 30 minutes.

APRICOTS AND PLUMS

Score a cross in the base of 2.5 kg (5 lb) apricots or 2.5 kg (5 lb) plums. Place in a heatproof bowl and cover with boiling water. Leave for 30 seconds, then transfer to cold water. Peel away the skins, halve and remove the stones. Make a sugar syrup by dissolving 2 cups (500 g/1 lb) sugar in

1 litre (32 fl oz) boiling water. Arrange the fruit in six 500 ml (16 fl oz) bottles. Follow the 10 steps to heat processing. Cook for 15 minutes.

PEACHES

Score a cross in the base of 2.5 kg (5 lb) slipstone peaches. Place in a heatproof bowl and cover with boiling water. Leave for 30 seconds, then transfer to cold water. Remove the skins, halve and remove the stones. Cut into 1.5 cm (5/8 inch) slices. Make a sugar syrup by dissolving 1 1/2 cups (375 g/12 oz) sugar in 1.125 litres (36 fl oz) boiling water. Arrange the fruit in six 500 ml (16 fl oz) bottles. Follow the 10 steps to heat processing. Cook for 15 minutes.

TOMATOES

Score a cross in the base of 2.5 kg (5 lb) Roma tomatoes. Place in a heatproof bowl and cover with boiling water. Leave for 30 seconds then transfer to cold water and peel the skin away. Make a brine of 1.5 litres (48 fl oz) water, 4 1/2 teaspoons salt and 1 table-spoon citric acid. Stir to dissolve over low heat for 2–3 minutes. Arrange the tomatoes in six 500 ml (16 fl oz) bottles. Follow the 10 steps to heat processing, using the brine instead of sugar syrup. Cook for 20 minutes.

Clockwise from top left: Pears; peaches; tomatoes; apricots; plums.

Pack the fruit tightly into the jars before covering with the hot sugar syrup.

Simmer the water throughout the cooking time, without allowing it to boil.

Protect your hands by wearing rubber gloves when removing the jars.

BLACK GRAPE JAM

Preparation time: 10 minutes
Total cooking time: 20 minutes
Makes 1 litre (32 fl oz)

1 kg (2 lb) seedless black
   grapes (see Note)
3 cups (750 g/1½ lb) sugar,
   warmed (see page 5)
2 tablespoons lemon juice
50 g (1¾ oz) jam-setting mixture

1 Remove the stems from the grapes and place in a large pan with ⅓ cup (80 ml/2¾ fl oz) water. Bring to the boil, then reduce the heat and simmer, covered, for 5 minutes.

2 Add the sugar and lemon juice and stir over low heat without boiling until all the sugar has dissolved.

3 Return to the boil and boil the jam rapidly for 10 minutes, stirring often. Remove any scum during cooking with a skimmer or slotted spoon. Add the jam-setting mixture and boil for a further 5 minutes. Remove any scum from the surface with a skimmer or slotted spoon.

4 Transfer to a heatproof jug and pour immediately into clean, warm jars, roughly dividing the whole grapes between the jars, and seal. Leave the jam to cool and, if possible, turn the jars on their ends every 15–20 minutes in order to ensure that the grapes are evenly distributed throughout the jam. Label and date. Store in a cool, dark place for 6–12 months. Refrigerate after opening for up to 6 weeks.

COOK'S FILE

Note: If using grapes with seeds, cut each grape in half and remove the seeds before continuing with the recipe.

Add the sugar and lemon juice to the grapes and stir until the sugar has dissolved.

Remove any scum from the surface before pouring into clean, warm jars.

Transfer the jam to a heatproof jug and pour or spoon into warm jars.

QUINCE CONSERVE

Preparation time: 20 minutes
Total cooking time: 1 hour
    30 minutes
Makes 2 litres (64 fl oz)

2 kg (4 lb) quinces (about 5)
³/4 cup (185 ml/6 fl oz)
    lemon juice
1.5 kg (3 lb) sugar, warmed
    (see page 5)

1 Put two small plates in the freezer. Cut each quince into quarters then peel, core and cut into small cubes.

Place the fruit in a large pan with 2 litres (64 fl oz) water and the lemon juice. Bring slowly to the boil, then reduce the heat and simmer, covered, for 1 hour, or until the fruit is soft.
2 Add the sugar and stir over low heat, without boiling, for 5 minutes, or until all the sugar has dissolved.
3 Return to the boil and boil, stirring often, for 25 minutes. Remove any scum during cooking with a skimmer or slotted spoon. When the conserve falls from a tilted wooden spoon in thick sheets without dripping, start testing for setting point.
4 Remove from the heat, place a little conserve onto one of the cold plates and

place in the freezer for 30 seconds. A skin will form on the surface and the conserve will wrinkle when pushed with your finger when setting point is reached. Remove any scum from the surface with a skimmer or slotted spoon.
5 Spoon immediately into clean, warm jars and seal. Turn upside down for 2 minutes, then invert and leave to cool. Label and date. Store in a cool, dark place for 6–12 months. Refrigerate after opening for up to 6 weeks.

COOK'S FILE

Note: The quinces will turn from their natural yellow to a beautiful, rich red during cooking.

Using a sharp knife, cut the peeled and cored quinces into small cubes.

After the sugar has dissolved, return the mixture to the boil for 25 minutes.

Remove any scum from the surface before spooning into clean, warm jars.

APPLE AND ROSE JELLY

Preparation time: 20 minutes +
  overnight draining
Total cooking time: 1 hour
Makes 1 cup (250 ml/8 fl oz)

1.5 kg (3 lb) apples
2 unsprayed roses
about 300 g (10 oz) caster
  sugar, warmed (see page 5)
2 teaspoons rose water

1 Chop the apples and put them in a pan with 1 litre (32 fl oz) water. Cook over low heat for 45 minutes, or until the apples have broken down into a purée.
2 Place a jelly bag in a bowl, cover with boiling water, drain and suspend the bag over a large heatproof bowl.
3 Ladle the purée into the bag. Do not push the fruit through the bag or the jelly will become cloudy. Cover the top of the bag loosely with a clean tea towel, without touching the fruit mixture. Allow the mixture to drip through the bag overnight, or until there is no liquid dripping through the cloth.
4 Put two small plates in the freezer. Pull the petals off the roses and wash them gently in cold water. Discard the pulp and measure the liquid. Pour the liquid into a large pan and add 1$\frac{1}{4}$ cups (310 g/10 oz) warmed sugar for every 2$\frac{1}{2}$ cups (600 ml/20 fl oz) liquid. Stir over low heat until all the sugar has dissolved. Bring to the boil and boil, stirring often, for 5–10 minutes. Remove any scum during cooking with a skimmer or slotted spoon. Start testing for setting point.
5 Remove from the heat, place a little jelly onto one of the cold plates and place in the freezer for 30 seconds. A skin will form on the surface and the jelly will

wrinkle when pushed with your finger when setting point is reached. Remove any scum from the surface. Stir in the rose petals and rose water, then leave to cool slightly until the jelly is beginning to set (this will ensure that the rose petals are suspended in the jelly).
6 Pour the jelly down the sides of clean, warm jars and seal. Turn upside down for 10 minutes, then

slowly invert to disperse the petals. Label and date. Store in a cool, dark place for 6–12 months. Refrigerate after opening for up to 6 weeks.

COOK'S FILE

Note: The amount of jelly will vary slightly according to how juicy the apples are and which types of apples are in season.

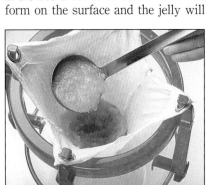

Ladle the apple purée into the jelly bag and leave overnight.

Stir in the rose petals and rose water once setting point is reached.

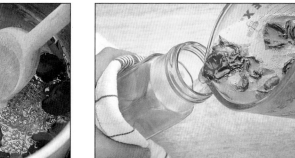

Pour the jelly down the sides of the clean, warm jars to avoid air bubbles.

DRIED APRICOT JAM

Preparation time: 10 minutes +
  overnight soaking
Total cooking time: 1 hour 10 minutes
Makes 1.75 litres (56 fl oz)

500 g (1 lb) dried apricots
1.5 kg (3 lb) sugar, warmed
  (see page 5)
1/2 cup (45 g/1 1/2 oz) flaked
  almonds

1 Place the dried apricots in a large non-metallic bowl. Add 2 litres (64 fl oz) water and leave to soak overnight.

2 Put two small plates in the freezer. Pour the apricots and water into a large pan. Bring to the boil, then reduce the heat and simmer, covered, for 45 minutes, or until the fruit is soft.

3 Add the sugar and stir over low heat, without boiling, for 5 minutes, or until all the sugar has dissolved. Return to the boil and boil, stirring often, for 20–25 minutes. Remove any scum during cooking with a skimmer or slotted spoon. Stir frequently across the base of the pan to prevent the jam from sticking. When the jam falls from a tilted wooden spoon in thick sheets without dripping, start testing for setting point.

4 Remove from the heat, place a little jam onto one of the cold plates and place in the freezer for 30 seconds. A skin will form on the surface and the jam will wrinkle when pushed with your finger when setting point is reached. Remove any scum. Add the flaked almonds.

5 Spoon immediately into clean, warm jars and seal. Turn upside down for 2 minutes, then invert and leave to cool. Label and date. Store in a cool, dark place for 6–12 months. Refrigerate after opening for up to 6 weeks.

After soaking the apricots overnight, add to a large pan, then cook until soft.

When the fruit is soft, add the warmed sugar to the pan and stir until dissolved.

When setting point is reached, a skin will form and the jam will wrinkle when pushed.

61

TOMATO AND PASSIONFRUIT JAM

Preparation time: 25 minutes
Total cooking time: 1 hour
Makes 2.5 litres (80 fl oz)

2 kg (4 lb) tomatoes
1 cup (250 g/8 oz)
    passionfruit pulp
    (about 10 passionfruit)
1/4 cup (60 ml/2 fl oz)
    lemon juice
2.5 kg (5 lb) sugar, warmed
    (see page 5)

1 Put two small plates in the freezer. Cut a cross at the base of the tomatoes, place in a large bowl, cover with boiling water and leave for 30 seconds, or until the skins start to peel away. Transfer to a bowl of icy cold water, remove the skins and roughly chop the tomatoes.
2 Put the passionfruit pulp, lemon juice, tomato and any juices in a large pan. Bring to the boil, then reduce the heat and simmer for 15 minutes, or until thick and pulpy.
3 Add the sugar and stir over low heat, without boiling, until all the sugar has dissolved. Return to the boil and boil for 30–40 minutes, stirring often. Remove any scum during cooking with a skimmer or slotted spoon. When the jam falls from a tilted wooden spoon in thick sheets without dripping, start testing for setting point.
4 Remove from the heat, place a little jam onto one of the cold plates and place in the freezer for 30 seconds. A skin will form on the surface and the jam will wrinkle when pushed with your finger when setting point is reached. Remove any scum from the surface.

5 Pour immediately into clean, warm jars, and seal. Turn upside down for 2 minutes, then invert and leave to cool. Label and date. Store in a cool, dark place for 6–12 months. Refrigerate after opening for up to 6 weeks.

Peel the tomato skins away from the cross at the base.

Simmer the mixture for 15 minutes, or until thick and pulpy.

Remove any scum from the surface before pouring into clean, warm jars.

FIG AND ORANGE JAM

Preparation time: 20 minutes
Total cooking time: 50 minutes
Makes 1.5 litres (48 fl oz)

1.5 kg (3 lb) fresh figs, chopped
¾ cup (185 ml/6 fl oz) orange juice
¼ cup (60 ml/2 fl oz) lemon juice
2 tablespoons sweet sherry
1 kg (2 lb) sugar, warmed
   (see page 5)

1 Put two small plates in the freezer. Place the figs in a large pan with the orange and lemon juice, and the sherry. Bring to the boil, then reduce the heat and simmer for 20 minutes, or until the figs are soft.

2 Add the sugar and stir over low heat, without boiling, until all the sugar has dissolved. Return to the boil and boil for 20–25 minutes, stirring often. Remove any scum during cooking with a skimmer or slotted spoon. When the jam falls from a tilted wooden spoon in thick sheets without dripping, start testing for setting point.

3 Remove from the heat, place a little jam onto one of the cold plates and place in the freezer for 30 seconds. A skin will form on the surface and the jam will wrinkle when pushed with your finger when setting point is reached. Remove any scum from the surface with a skimmer or slotted spoon.

4 Pour immediately into clean, warm jars and seal. Turn upside down for 2 minutes, then invert and leave to cool. Label and date. Store in a cool, dark place for 6–12 months. Refrigerate after opening for up to 6 weeks.

COOK'S FILE

Note: Either dark- or green-skinned figs can be used in this recipe.

Reduce the heat and simmer the mixture for 20 minutes, or until the figs are tender.

Test for setting point when the jam falls in thick sheets from a spoon without dripping.

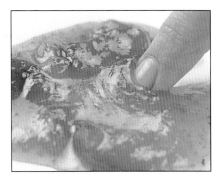

Setting point is reached when the jam wrinkles when pushed with your finger.

SAVOURY JAMS AND PRESERVES

GREEN MANGO CHUTNEY

Preparation time: 20 minutes
Total cooking time: 50 minutes
Makes 3 cups (750 ml/24 fl oz)

6 medium (2.6 kg/5¼ lb)
    firm green mangoes
1 large onion, finely chopped
²/3 cup (170 ml/5½ fl oz)
    white vinegar
½ cup (115 g/4 oz) firmly
    packed soft brown sugar
¾ cup (185 g/6 oz) sugar
2 teaspoons ground ginger
2 teaspoons garam marsala

1 Remove the peel from the mangoes. Cut the cheeks from the rounded side of each mango and the small amount of flesh around the sides of the seed. Chop the flesh into 1 cm (½ inch) pieces and place in a large pan.
2 Add the remaining ingredients and 1 teaspoon salt to the pan. Stir over medium heat, without boiling, for 5 minutes, or until all the sugar has dissolved.
3 Bring to the boil, then reduce the heat and simmer for about 45 minutes, or until the mixture is very thick and pulpy. Stir often during cooking to prevent the chutney from sticking and burning on the bottom, especially towards the end of the cooking time.
4 Spoon immediately into clean, warm jars and seal. Turn the jars upside down for 2 minutes, then invert and leave to cool. Label and date. Leave for 1 month before opening to allow the flavours to develop. Store in a cool, dark place for up to 12 months. Refrigerate after opening for up to 6 weeks.

COOK'S FILE

Note: This chutney is a traditional accompaniment to Indian-style dishes. Choose firm, green mangoes without bruises or blemishes.

Remove the peel and chop the mango flesh into small pieces.

Simmer the mixture for 45 minutes, or until thick and pulpy.

CHOW CHOW

Preparation time: 30 minutes
Total cooking time: 20 minutes
Makes 2.75 litres (88 fl oz)

650 g (1 lb/5 oz) cauliflower,
    cut into small florets
1 Lebanese cucumber, peeled,
    seeded and cut into
    2 cm (3/4 inch) cubes
375 g (12 oz) green beans,
    trimmed and cut into
    3 cm (1 1/4 inch) lengths
1 red capsicum, cut into
    cubes
1 green capsicum, cut into cubes
1 litre (32 fl oz) cider vinegar
1 cup (230 g/7 1/2 oz) firmly
    packed soft brown sugar
2 tablespoons mustard powder
2 tablespoons yellow
    mustard seeds
2 teaspoons ground turmeric
pinch cayenne pepper
1/2 cup (60 g/2 oz) plain flour
420 g (14 oz) can red kidney
    beans, rinsed and drained
310 g (10 oz) can corn
    kernels, drained

1 Blanch the cauliflower florets, cucumber, beans and capsicum separately in boiling water. Drain and cool quickly under cold running water. Set aside.

2 Reserve 1 cup (250 ml/8 fl oz) of the vinegar. Combine the remaining vinegar with the sugar, mustard powder and seeds, turmeric and cayenne pepper in a large pan. Stir over low heat to dissolve the sugar.

3 Whisk the reserved vinegar and the flour together in a bowl. Add to the pan and whisk over medium heat for 5 minutes, or until the mixture boils and thickens. Add the blanched vegetables, kidney beans and corn kernels. Mix thoroughly, bring to the boil, and cook, stirring often, for another 5 minutes.

4 Spoon immediately into clean, warm jars and seal. Turn upside down for 2 minutes, then invert and leave to cool. Label and date. Leave for 1 month before opening to allow the flavours to develop. Store in a cool, dark place for up to 12 months. Refrigerate after opening for up to 6 weeks.

Scrape out the seeds of the Lebanese cucumber with a teaspoon.

Add the whisked mixture to the pan and whisk over medium heat.

NECTARINE AND LEMON GRASS CHUTNEY

Preparation time: 25 minutes
Total cooking time: 1 hour
Makes 1.25 litres (40 fl oz)

3 large green chillies
3 stalks lemon grass,
    white part only
1.5 kg (3 lb) nectarines, stones
    removed, roughly chopped
3 cloves garlic, finely chopped
2 tablespoons grated fresh ginger
1 large onion, chopped

2 teaspoons ground coriander
2 cups (500 ml/16 fl oz) white
    wine vinegar
1½ cups (280 g/9 oz) lightly
    packed soft brown sugar

1 Cut the chillies in half, remove the seeds from two and finely slice all the chillies. Bruise the lemon grass with the back of a knife and slice finely.
2 Place all the ingredients in a large pan and add 1 teaspoon salt. Stir over low heat for 5 minutes, or until all the sugar has dissolved.
3 Bring to the boil, then reduce the heat and simmer for 45–50 minutes, or until the chutney is thick and pulpy. Stir often to prevent the chutney from sticking or burning on the bottom.
4 Spoon immediately into clean, warm jars and seal. Turn the jars upside down for 2 minutes, then invert and leave to cool. Label and date. Leave for 1 month before opening to allow the flavours to develop. Store in a cool, dark place for up to 12 months. Refrigerate after opening for up to 6 weeks.

COOK'S FILE

Note: Wear gloves when handling the chillies to protect your fingers.

Wearing gloves to protect your hands, remove the seeds from two chillies.

Using only the white part, bruise the lemon grass with the back of a knife.

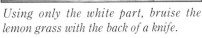

Simmer the chutney for 45–50 minutes, or until it is thick and pulpy.

CHILLI AND RED CAPSICUM RELISH

Preparation time: 15 minutes
Total cooking time: 1 hour
Makes 1.25 litres (40 fl oz)

4 large red capsicums
2 large onions, roughly
    chopped
1 red chilli
2 cloves garlic
2 cups (500 ml/16 fl oz)
    white vinegar
1.5 kg (3 lb) sugar,
    approximately

1 Quarter the capsicums and remove the seeds and white membrane. Roughly chop and place in a food processor or blender with the onion, chilli, garlic and some salt. You may need to do this in batches. Process until smooth and place in a large pan.
2 Add the vinegar, bring to the boil and boil for 10–15 minutes, or until tender. Measure the capsicum mixture and measure an equal amount of sugar. Add the sugar, stirring until all the sugar has dissolved, and then slowly bring to the boil. Brush down the sides of the pan with a wet brush to remove any undissolved sugar crystals. Remove any scum during cooking with a skimmer or slotted spoon.

3 Boil for 15 minutes, stirring often, then reduce the heat and simmer for 30 minutes, or until the relish is thick and pulpy.
4 Spoon immediately into clean, warm jars and seal. Turn the jars upside down for 2 minutes, then invert and cool. Label and date. Leave for 1 month before opening to allow the flavours to develop. Store in a cool, dark place for up to 12 months. Refrigerate after opening for up to 6 weeks.

COOK'S FILE

Note: Brushing the sides of the pan dissolves any sugar crystals which, if left, could cause the relish to crystallize when chilled.

Quarter the capsicum and remove the seeds and white membrane.

Process the capsicum, onion, chilli, garlic and salt in a food processor or blender.

Brush down the sides of the pan to remove any undissolved sugar crystals.

ONION AND THYME MARMALADE

Preparation time: 20 minutes
Total cooking time: 1 hour 20 minutes
Makes 1 litre (32 fl oz)

2 kg (4 lb) onions, cut into rings
3 cups (750 ml/24 fl oz) malt
    vinegar
6 black peppercorns
2 bay leaves
3¹/₂ cups (805 g/1 lb 10 oz) firmly
    packed soft brown sugar

2 tablespoons fresh thyme leaves
10 x 3 cm (1¹/₄ inch) sprigs
    fresh thyme

1 Place the onion in a large pan with the vinegar. Put the peppercorns and bay leaves on a square of muslin and tie securely with string. Add to the pan. Bring to the boil, then reduce the heat and simmer for 40–45 minutes, or until the onion is very soft.
2 Add the sugar, thyme leaves and 1 teaspoon salt. Stir until all the sugar has dissolved. Bring to the boil, then reduce the heat and simmer, for

20–30 minutes, or until thick and syrupy. Skim any scum off the surface during cooking with a skimmer or slotted spoon. Discard the muslin bag and stir in the fresh thyme sprigs.
3 Spoon the onion pulp immediately into clean, warm jars, then pour in the syrup and seal the jars. Turn upside down for 2 minutes, then invert and leave to cool. Label and date. Leave for 1 month before opening to allow the flavours to develop. Store in a cool, dark place for up to 12 months. Refrigerate after opening for up to 6 weeks.

Peel the onions and then cut them into rings.

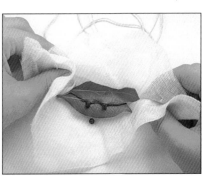

Put the peppercorns and bay leaves on a piece of muslin and tie securely.

When the mixture is thick and syrupy, remove the muslin bag with tongs.

BANANA, TAMARIND AND DATE CHUTNEY

Preparation time: 25 minutes
Total cooking time: 45 minutes
Makes 1.5 litres (48 fl oz)

125 g (4 oz) tamarind pulp
1/3 cup (90 g/3 oz) caster sugar
1 teaspoon ground cumin
1/2 teaspoon cayenne pepper
2 tablespoons grated fresh
   ginger
250 g (8 oz) pitted dates, chopped
1/2 cup (60 g/2 oz) slivered
   almonds
8 firm ripe bananas, chopped

1 Put the tamarind pulp in a bowl with 3 cups (750 ml/24 fl oz) boiling water. Cool, then break up with a fork. Pour into a sieve placed over a bowl and press out the liquid. Discard the seeds.
2 Put the liquid in a large pan with the sugar, cumin, cayenne pepper and 1 teaspoon salt. Stir over low heat until all the sugar has dissolved.
3 Add the ginger, dates and almonds. Bring to the boil, then reduce the heat and simmer for 10 minutes. Add the banana and cook, stirring often, for 30 minutes, or until soft and pulpy.
4 Spoon immediately into clean, warm jars. Use a metal skewer to remove any air bubbles and seal. Turn upside down for 2 minutes, then invert and leave to cool. Label and date. Leave for 1 month before opening to allow the flavours to develop. Store in a cool, dark place for up to 12 months. Refrigerate after opening for up to 6 weeks.

COOK'S FILE

Note: Tamarind pulp is available in most Asian grocery stores.

Put the tamarind pulp in a bowl with boiling water and leave to cool.

Put the strained liquid in a large pan with the sugar, cumin, salt and cayenne.

Cook the mixture until it is thick and pulpy, stirring frequently.

CHILLI JAM

Preparation time: 15 minutes
Total cooking time: 30 minutes
Makes 1 litre (32 fl oz)

500 g (1 lb) red capsicums
120 g (4 oz) red chillies
1¼ cups (315 ml/10 fl oz) white
    vinegar
4 cups (1 kg/2 lb) sugar
1 cup (185 g/6 oz) lightly
    packed soft brown sugar

1 Remove the seeds and membrane from the capsicum and chilli. Cut the capsicum into large flattish pieces, and cook skin-side-up under a hot grill until the skin blackens and blisters. Place in a plastic bag and cool, then remove the skin.

2 Put the capsicum and chilli in a food processor with ¼ cup (60 ml/2 fl oz) vinegar and process until finely chopped, in batches if necessary.

3 Put the capsicum and chilli mixture in a large pan and add the remaining vinegar. Bring to the boil, then reduce the heat and simmer for 8 minutes. Remove from the heat. Add the sugars and stir for 5 minutes, or until all the sugar has dissolved, then return to the heat and boil for 5–10 minutes, or until it has thickened slightly.

4 Spoon immediately into clean, warm jars and seal. Turn the jars upside down for 2 minutes, then invert and leave to cool. Label and date. Leave for 1 month before opening to allow the flavours to develop. Store in a cool, dark place for up to 12 months. Refrigerate after opening for up to 6 weeks.

Cook the capsicums, skin-side-up, under a hot grill until the skin blackens and blisters.

Put the capsicum and chilli mixture in a large pan and add the white vinegar.

Spoon the jam immediately into clean, warm jars and seal.

71

BLUEBERRY RELISH

Preparation time: 15 minutes
Total cooking time: 1 hour
Makes 3 cups (750 ml/24 fl oz)

1 kg (2 lb) blueberries
2 cups (500 g/1 lb) sugar
3/4 cup (185 ml/6 fl oz)
   white wine vinegar
1 teaspoon cayenne pepper
1/2 teaspoon ground allspice
   (pimento)
1/4 teaspoon ground cinnamon
1/4 cup (60 ml/2 fl oz) lemon juice
   (reserve any pips and rind)

1 Place the blueberries in a large pan with the sugar, vinegar, cayenne pepper, allspice, cinnamon, lemon juice, 1 teaspoon salt and 1/2 cup (125 ml/ 4 fl oz) water. Roughly chop the rind of half a lemon and, with the pips, place onto a square of muslin and tie securely with string. Add to the pan.
2 Stir over low heat for 5 minutes, or until all the sugar has dissolved.
3 Bring to the boil, then reduce the heat and simmer, stirring often, for 50–55 minutes, or until the relish is thick and syrupy.
4 Spoon immediately into clean, warm jars and seal. Turn the jars upside down for 2 minutes, then invert and leave to cool. Label and date. Leave for 1 month before opening to allow the flavours to develop. Store in a cool, dark place for up to 12 months. Refrigerate after opening for up to 6 weeks.

COOK'S FILE

Note: Blueberries are delicate fruit, so be careful not to overcook them or they will break up and fall apart.

Place the lemon rind and pips onto a square of muslin and tie with string.

Simmer for 50–55 minutes, stirring often, or until thick and syrupy.

Spoon the relish immediately into clean, warm jars and seal.

RED WINE JELLY

Preparation time: 20 minutes
+ overnight draining
Total cooking time: 1 hour 30 minutes
Makes 1.5 litres (48 fl oz)

1 kg (2 lb) green apples
2 red apples
4 whole allspice (pimento)
4 whole cloves
2 cups (500 ml/16 fl oz) good-
  quality red wine (see Note)
1 tablespoon lemon juice
1 kg (2 lb) caster sugar, warmed
  (see page 5)

1 Cut the apples into quarters, including the skin and cores. Place in a large pan with the allspice, cloves and 1 litre (32 fl oz) water. Bring slowly to the boil, then reduce the heat and simmer, covered, for 40 minutes, or until the apple is soft and pulpy.
2 Place a jelly bag in a bowl, cover with boiling water, drain and suspend the bag over a large heatproof bowl.
3 Pour the fruit and liquid into the bag. Do not push the fruit through the bag or the jelly will become cloudy. Cover the top of the bag loosely with a clean tea towel, without touching the fruit mixture. Allow the mixture to drip through the bag overnight, or until there is no liquid dripping through the cloth.
4 Place two small plates in the freezer. Discard the pulp. Add the wine and lemon juice to the liquid, and measure. Pour the liquid into a large pan, and heat until boiling. Add 1 cup (250 g/8 oz) of the warmed sugar for each 1 cup (250 ml/8 fl oz) of liquid and stir over low heat until the sugar has dissolved. Bring to the boil

and boil rapidly, stirring often, for 40 minutes. Remove any scum during cooking with a skimmer or slotted spoon. Start testing for setting point.
5 Remove from the heat and test for setting point by placing a little jelly on one of the plates. A skin will form on the surface and the jelly will wrinkle when pushed with your finger when setting point is reached.
6 Pour immediately down the sides of clean, warm jars. Turn upside

down for 2 minutes, then invert and leave to cool. Label and date. Keep in a cool, dark place for 6–12 months. Refrigerate after opening for up to 6 weeks.

COOK'S FILE

Note: Cabernet sauvignon or shiraz are suitable wines. Red wine jelly can be served with beef, pork, lamb or ham, as well as meat or poultry terrines and pâtés, or cheese.

Add the allspice and cloves to the quartered apples in the pan.

Cover the top of the jelly bag with a clean tea towel, without touching the mixture.

Bring to the boil, and then add the warmed sugar.

ROAST PEACH CHUTNEY

Preparation time: 30 minutes
Total cooking time: 2 hours
Makes 1.25 litres (40 fl oz)

2 kg (4 lb) ripe slipstone peaches
2 onions, thinly sliced
2 cloves garlic, crushed
1½ cups (375 g/12 oz) sugar
2½ cups (600 ml/20 fl oz)
    cider vinegar
1 tablespoon yellow mustard
    seeds
2 cinnamon sticks
1 teaspoon ground ginger

1 Preheat the oven to hot 210°C (415°F/Gas 6–7). Score a cross in the base of the peaches, place them in a heatproof bowl and cover with boiling water. Leave for 30 seconds, then cover with cold water and peel the skin away from the cross. Cut the peaches in half and remove the stone.
2 Line 2–3 rectangular pans with baking paper. Place the peaches in a single layer on the paper and roast for 30 minutes, or until they start to brown on the edges. (A lot of juice will come out of the peaches.) Tip the peaches and any juices into a large pan, and add the onion, garlic, sugar, vinegar, mustard seeds, cinnamon

sticks and ginger. Stir over heat until all the sugar has dissolved.
3 Return to the boil, then reduce the heat and simmer for 1¼–1½ hours, or until the chutney is thick and pulpy. Stir occasionally to break up the peaches and prevent the mixture from sticking to the bottom of the pan. Remove the cinnamon sticks.
4 Spoon immediately into clean, warm jars and seal. Turn upside down for 2 minutes, then invert and leave to cool. Label and date. Leave for 1 month before opening to allow the flavours to develop. Store in a cool, dark place for up to 12 months. Refrigerate after opening for up to 6 weeks.

Peel the skin away from the peaches, starting at the cross.

Roast the peaches for 30 minutes, or until they start to brown on the edges.

Reduce the heat and simmer until the chutney is thick and pulpy.

TOMATO SAUCE

Preparation time: 25 minutes
Total cooking time: 2 hours
Makes 1.5 litres (48 fl oz)

2.5 kg (5 lb) firm, ripe
    tomatoes
1 large onion
2 teaspoons black peppercorns
2 teaspoons whole cloves
2 teaspoons whole allspice
    (pimento)
1½ tablespoons tomato paste
4 cloves garlic, crushed
2 teaspoons ground ginger
¼ teaspoon cayenne pepper
2½ cups (600 ml/20 fl oz)
    white wine or cider vinegar
1 cup (250 g/1 lb) sugar

1 Roughly chop the tomatoes and onion. Place the peppercorns, whole cloves and allspice on a square of muslin and tie securely with string.
2 Place the tomato and onion in a large pan with the muslin bag, tomato paste, garlic, ginger, cayenne pepper, vinegar and 1 teaspoon salt. Bring slowly to the boil, then reduce the heat and simmer for 45 minutes.
3 Add the sugar and stir over low heat for 5 minutes, or until all the sugar has dissolved.
4 Bring to the boil, then reduce the heat and simmer for 1 hour, or until the sauce is thick and pulpy. Stir frequently during cooking and watch that the mixture does not burn. Discard the muslin bag.
5 Place the mixture in a coarse sieve set over a large bowl, in batches if necessary. Use a metal spoon to press all the juices firmly from the pulp. Discard the pulp and return the juice to

the clean pan. Gently reheat the mixture for 10 minutes, then pour immediately into clean, warm jars or bottles and seal. Turn upside down for 2 minutes, then invert and leave to

cool. Label and date. Leave for 1 month before opening to allow the flavours to develop. Store in a cool, dark place for up to 12 months. Refrigerate after opening for up to 6 weeks.

Put the peppercorns, cloves and allspice in a muslin bag and add to the pan.

Simmer the sauce for an hour, or until it is thick and pulpy.

Press the sauce through a coarse sieve, extracting all the juice from the pulp.

PRESERVED LEMONS

Preparation time: 1 hour +
  6 weeks standing
Total cooking time: nil
Makes a 2 litre jar (64 fl oz)

8–12 small thin-skinned lemons
1 cup (315 g/10 oz) rock salt
2 cups (500 ml/16 fl oz) lemon
    juice (8–10 lemons)
1/2 teaspoon black peppercorns
1 bay leaf
1 tablespoon olive oil

1 Scrub the lemons under warm running water with a soft bristle brush to remove the wax coating. Cut into quarters, leaving the base attached at the stem end. Gently open each lemon, remove any visible pips and pack 1 tablespoon of the salt against the cut edges of each lemon. Push the lemons back into shape and pack tightly into a 2 litre (64 fl oz) jar with a clip or tight-fitting lid. (Depending on the size of the lemons, you may not need all 12. They should be firmly packed and fill the jar.)
2 Add 1 cup (250 ml/8 fl oz) of the lemon juice, the remaining rock salt, the peppercorns and bay leaf to the jar. Fill the jar to the top with the remaining lemon juice. Seal and shake to combine all the ingredients. Leave in a cool, dark place for 6 weeks, inverting each week. (In warm weather, store in the refrigerator.) The liquid will be cloudy initially, but will clear by the fourth week.
3 To test if the lemons are preserved, cut through the centre of one of the lemon quarters. If the pith is still white, the lemons are not ready. Re-seal and leave for another week before testing again.
4 Once the lemons are preserved, cover the brine with a layer of olive oil. Replace the oil each time you remove some of the lemon.

COOK'S FILE

Storage time: Preserved lemons can be stored for up to 6 months in a cool, dark place.
Hint: Serve the lemons with grilled meats or use to flavour couscous, stuffings, tagines and casseroles. Only the rind is used in cooking. Discard the flesh, rinse and finely slice or chop the rind before adding to the dish.

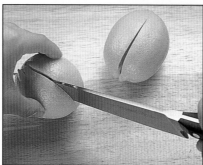

Cut the lemons into quarters, leaving the base attached at the stem end.

Pack 1 tablespoon of salt against the cut edges of each lemon.

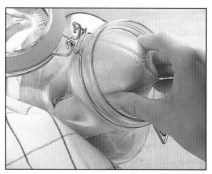

Push the lemons back into shape and pack tightly into a 2 litre (64 fl oz) jar.

Pour the remaining lemon juice into the jar, filling it to the top.

RED CAPSICUM RELISH

Preparation time: 40 minutes
Total cooking time: 1 hour 50 minutes
Makes 2 cups (500 ml/16 fl oz)

1 kg (2 lb) red capsicums
1½ cups (375 ml/12 fl oz)
    red wine vinegar
2 teaspoons black mustard seeds
2 red onions, thinly sliced
4 cloves garlic, chopped
1 teaspoon grated fresh ginger
2 apples, peeled, cored and grated
1 teaspoon black peppercorns
1 cup (230 g/7½ oz) firmly
    packed soft brown sugar

1 Remove the seeds and membranes and thinly slice the capsicums. Put in a large pan with the vinegar, mustard seeds, onion, garlic, ginger and apple. Place the peppercorns on a square of muslin, tie securely with string, and add to the pan. Simmer for 30 minutes, or until the capsicum is soft.

2 Add the sugar and stir over low heat, without boiling, until all the sugar has dissolved. Bring to the boil, stirring often, then reduce the heat and simmer, for 1¼ hours, or until the relish is thick and pulpy. Discard the muslin bag.

3 Spoon immediately into clean, warm jars and seal. Turn the jars upside down for 2 minutes, then invert and leave to cool. Label and date. Leave for 1 month before opening to allow the flavours to develop. Store in a cool, dark place for up to 12 months. Refrigerate after opening for up to 6 weeks.

Remove the seeds and membranes and thinly slice the capsicum.

Tie the peppercorns securely in a square of muslin and add to the pan.

Simmer the relish until it is thick and the vegetables have softened.

INDIAN LIME PICKLE

Preparation time: 20 minutes + cooling
Total cooking time: 15 minutes
Makes 1 litre (32 fl oz)

10 firm yellow/pale green limes
3/4 cup (185 ml/6 fl oz) oil
1 teaspoon fenugreek seeds
3/4 teaspoon ground turmeric
3 teaspoons chilli powder
1 teaspoon asafoetida powder

1 Wash the limes and dry thoroughly. Heat 1/4 cup (60 ml/2 fl oz) oil in a pan. Add 2 limes and cook over low heat, turning often, for 2 minutes. Remove and repeat until all the limes are done. Do not allow the skin to turn brown. Cool, then cut each lime into eight wedges and cut each wedge into three. Discard the seeds and reserve any juice.
2 In a dry pan, heat the fenugreek seeds for 1 minute, or until the colour lightens. Take care not to burn the seeds as this will make the pickle bitter. Grind to a fine powder in a mortar and pestle or spice mill.
3 Heat the remaining oil in a heavy-based pan. Add the turmeric, chilli powder, asafoetida and 1 tablespoon salt. Stir quickly and add the limes and reserved juice. Turn off the heat, add the ground fenugreek and stir well.
4 Spoon immediately into clean, warm jars. Pour a thin layer of warmed oil into each bottle. Seal, label and date. Leave for 1 month before opening to allow the flavours to develop. Store in a cool, dark place for up to 12 months. Refrigerate after opening for up to 6 weeks.

COOK'S FILE

Note: Dark green limes are too acidic so use pale green/yellow ones. The rind softens with time. Asafoetida powder is a dried plant resin with a strong garlicky smell and is available from Indian spice stores.

Cook 2 limes at a time in the heated oil, turning often.

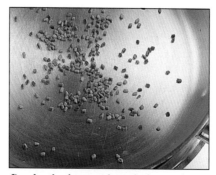

Dry-fry the fenugreek seeds for 1 minute, or until the colour lightens.

Add the turmeric, chilli powder, asafoetida powder and salt to the heated oil.

THAI SWEET CHILLI SAUCE

Preparation time: 30 minutes
Total cooking time: 20 minutes
Makes 3 cups (750 ml/24 fl oz)

150 g (5 oz) medium–large
   fresh red chillies
1²/₃ cups (210 g/7 oz)
   sultanas
3 cloves garlic, chopped
3 cm (1¹/₂ inches) finely
   grated fresh ginger
1 cup (250 ml/8 fl oz)
   white vinegar
1²/₃ cups (410 g/13 oz)
   sugar
²/₃ cup (155 g/5 oz) firmly
   packed soft brown sugar
1 tablespoon fish sauce

1 Wearing latex or rubber gloves to protect your hands, cut the chillies in half and remove the seeds.
2 Combine the chilli, sultanas, garlic, ginger and ¹/₄ cup (60 ml/2 fl oz) of the vinegar in a food processor or blender and process until smooth.
3 Place the chilli mixture in a large pan, stir in the remaining vinegar, white and brown sugar, fish sauce, ¹/₄ teaspoon salt and 100 ml (6¹/₂ fl oz) water. Bring to the boil, stirring until all the sugar has dissolved, then reduce the heat and simmer, stirring often, for 15 minutes, or until the mixture is a slightly thick, syrupy consistency.
4 Pour immediately into clean, warm jars or bottles and seal. Turn the jars upside down for 2 minutes, then invert and cool. Label and date. Leave for 1 month before opening to allow the flavours to develop. Store in a cool, dark place for up to 12 months. Refrigerate after opening for up to 6 weeks.

COOK'S FILE

Note: This sauce is quite sweet, yet has a good bite. If you prefer a milder sauce, you can adjust the amount of chilli to your taste. The seeds contain the most heat, so remember to remove these. Wearing gloves helps prevent any irritation to sensitive skin which can sometimes occur when dealing with chillies.

Wearing gloves to protect your hands, remove the seeds from the chillies.

Add the remaining ingredients and stir until the sugar has dissolved.

GREEN TOMATO PICKLES

Preparation time: 25 minutes +
   overnight soaking
Total cooking time: 40 minutes
Makes 1.25 litres (40 fl oz)

1.25 kg (2¹/₂ lb) green tomatoes
2 onions
¹/₂ cup (120 g/4 oz) cooking salt
1 cup (250 g/8 oz) sugar
2 cups (500 ml/16 fl oz) cider
   vinegar
¹/₂ cup (60 g/2 oz) sultanas
¹/₂ teaspoon mixed spice

¹/₂ teaspoon ground cinnamon
2 teaspoons curry powder
pinch cayenne pepper
2 teaspoons cornflour

1 Slice the tomatoes and onions into thin rounds. Combine with the salt in a large non-metallic bowl and add enough water to cover. Place a small plate on top of the vegetables to keep them submerged. Leave to stand overnight.
2 Drain the tomato and onion and rinse well. Place in a large pan and add the sugar, vinegar, sultanas and spices. Stir over low heat for 5 minutes, or

until all the sugar has dissolved.
3 Bring to the boil, then reduce the heat and simmer for 30 minutes, stirring often, or until the vegetables are soft.
4 Add 2 teaspoons water to the cornflour, mix well and and stir into the mixture. Stir over medium heat until it boils and thickens.
5 Spoon immediately into clean, warm jars and seal. Turn the jars upside down for 2 minutes, then invert and leave to cool. Label and date. Leave for 1 month before opening to allow the flavours to develop. Store in a cool, dark place for up to 12 months. Refrigerate after opening for up to 6 weeks.

Using a sharp knife, cut the green tomatoes into thin rounds.

Cover with an upturned plate to keep submerged and leave to soak overnight.

Stir the mixture well after adding the cornflour until it boils and thickens.

BEETROOT RELISH

Preparation time: 25 minutes
Total cooking time: 35 minutes
Makes 1 litre (32 fl oz)

750 g (1¹/₂ lb) fresh beetroot, peeled and coarsely grated
1 onion, chopped
400 g (13 oz) green apples, peeled, cored and chopped
1²/₃ cups (410 ml/13 fl oz) white wine vinegar
¹/₂ cup (95 g/3 oz) lightly packed soft brown sugar
¹/₂ cup (125 g/4 oz) sugar
2 tablespoons lemon juice

1 Place all the ingredients and 2 teaspoons salt in a large pan and stir over low heat, without boiling, until all the sugar has dissolved. Bring to the boil and boil, stirring often, for 20–30 minutes, or until the beetroot and onion are tender and the relish is reduced and thickened.
2 Spoon immediately into clean, warm jars, and seal. Turn upside down for 2 minutes, then invert and leave to cool. Label and date. Leave for 1 month before opening to allow the flavours to develop. Store in a cool, dark place for up to 12 months. Refrigerate after opening for up to 6 weeks.

COOK'S FILE

Variation: For a little extra kick, you can stir 1–2 tablespoons bottled horseradish into the mixture.
Serving suggestion: Serve with lamb hamburgers or cold meats.

Peel the fresh beetroot, then coarsely grate each one.

Place all the ingredients in a large pan and stir over low heat.

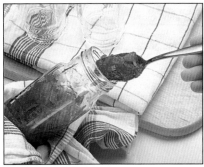

Spoon the thickened relish into clean, warm jars.

OKRA PICKLES

Preparation time: 20 minutes +
   25 minutes standing
Total cooking time: 10 minutes
Makes 2 cups (500 ml/16 fl oz)

1²/₃ cups (410 ml/13 fl oz)
   cider vinegar
1 teaspoon coriander seeds
1 teaspoon mustard seeds
1 cinnamon stick
4–6 dried small red chillies
2 tablespoons soft brown sugar
1 onion, chopped
500 g (1 lb) small okra, chopped
   into 1 cm (¹/₂ inch) pieces

1 Place the vinegar, spices, chillies, sugar and 1¹/₂ tablespoons water in a large pan and bring to the boil. Reduce the heat and simmer for 5 minutes, then remove from the heat, cover and infuse for 25 minutes.

2 Strain the vinegar mixture, reserving the chillies, then return to the pan. You will need about 1¹/₂ cups (375 ml/12 fl oz) of liquid. Add the onion and okra, 2 tablespoons salt and bring to the boil. Reduce the heat and simmer over low heat for 5 minutes, or until the okra is half cooked and there is no more of the sliminess that the okra releases. Skim off any scum during cooking with a skimmer or slotted spoon.

3 Strain the okra and onion mixture, reserving the liquid, and pack immediately into clean, warm jars, adding two of the reserved chillies to each jar. Fill the jars with the reserved pickling liquid and seal. Turn upside down for 2 minutes, then invert and leave to cool. Label and date. Leave for 1 month before opening to allow the flavours to develop. Store in a cool, dark place for up to 12 months. Refrigerate after opening for up to 6 weeks.

COOK'S FILE

Note: Use small okra as the larger, older ones tend to be more fibrous. The okra will start to absorb the liquid after 1–2 weeks.

Trim a small amount from the ends of the okra and then chop into small pieces.

Strain the vinegar mixture and reserve the chillies.

Spoon the strained okra and onion mixture into the warm jars.

SPICY PUMPKIN CHUTNEY

Preparation time: 20 minutes
Total cooking time: 55 minutes
Makes 1 litre (32 fl oz)

1 kg (2 lb) pumpkin, peeled
    and cut into small chunks
2 tablespoons oil
2 teaspoons cumin seeds
1/2 teaspoon ground cinnamon
1/2 teaspoon ground coriander
1 onion, chopped
2 cloves garlic, crushed
1/2 cup (60 g/2 oz) sultanas

1/3 cup (80 g/2¾ oz) firmly
    packed soft brown sugar
1/2 cup (125 ml/4 fl oz)
    malt vinegar
3/4 cup (185 ml/6 fl oz) orange juice
1 tablespoon chopped fresh
    coriander leaves

1 Preheat the oven to moderately hot 200°C (400°F/Gas 6). Place the pumpkin in a baking dish and drizzle with the oil. Bake for 40 minutes.
2 Put the pumpkin and the remaining ingredients, except the coriander leaves, in a large pan. Add 1/2 teaspoon salt and bring to the boil. Reduce the heat and simmer for 10–15 minutes, stirring

often, or until the mixture thickens.
3 Gently stir in the coriander and remove from the heat. Spoon immediately into clean, warm jars and seal. Turn upside down for 2 minutes, then invert and leave to cool. Label and date. Leave for 1 month before opening to allow the flavours to develop. Store in a cool, dark place for up to 12 months. Refrigerate after opening for up to 6 weeks.

COOK'S FILE

Note: To get a thick and chunky mixture, use harder pumpkin varieties that take longer to cook, such as Queensland Blue or Jarrahdale.

Place the pumpkin pieces in a baking dish and drizzle with oil.

Combine the baked pumpkin with the remaining ingredients.

When the mixture has thickened, stir in the fresh coriander.

PLUM SAUCE

Preparation time: 20 minutes
Total cooking time: 1 hour
Makes 1 litre (32 fl oz)

1 large green apple
2 red chillies
1.25 kg (2½ lb) blood plums,
   halved
2 cups (460 g/14½ oz) firmly
   packed soft brown sugar
1½ cups (375 ml/12 fl oz)
   white wine vinegar
1 onion, grated
¼ cup (60 ml/2 fl oz)
   soy sauce
2 tablespoons fresh ginger,
   finely chopped
2 cloves garlic, crushed

1 Peel, core and chop the apple and place in a large pan with ½ cup (125 ml/4 fl oz) water. Cover and simmer for 10 minutes, or until the apple is soft. Cut the chillies in half lengthways. Remove the seeds and chop finely. Add the plums, sugar, vinegar, onion, soy sauce, ginger, garlic and the chilli.

2 Bring the mixture to the boil and cook, uncovered, over low–medium heat for 45 minutes. Stir the mixture often throughout the cooking process. Remove the sauce from the pan and press it through a coarse strainer set over a large bowl using a wooden spoon. Discard the plum stones. Rinse the pan. Put the sauce back in the clean pan and return to the heat.

3 Cook the sauce rapidly while stirring until it has thickened slightly—the sauce will thicken even further on cooling.

4 Pour immediately into clean, warm jars and seal. Turn the jars upside down for 2 minutes, then invert and leave to cool. Label and date. Leave for 1 month before opening to allow the flavours to develop. Store in a cool, dark place for up to 12 months. Refrigerate after opening for up to 6 weeks.

COOK'S FILE

Serving suggestion: Plum sauce is delicious with beef or pork spareribs, Chinese barbecued pork and duck.

Press the sauce through a strainer with a wooden spoon.

Cook the sauce rapidly while stirring, until it has thickened slightly.

SAGE JELLY

Preparation time: 15 minutes +
overnight draining
Total cooking time: 1 hour
Makes 3 cups (750 ml/24 fl oz)

1 kg (2 lb) green apples
3/4 cup (15 g/1/2 oz) fresh
   sage leaves
3 cups (750 g/11/2 lb) caster
   sugar, approximately
1/2 cup (125 ml/4 fl oz)
   lemon juice
1/4 cup (10 g/1/4 oz) firmly
   packed shredded fresh
   sage leaves

1 Chop the apples, including the skin and cores. Place in a large pan with the sage leaves and 3 cups (750 ml/ 24 fl oz) water. Bring slowly to the boil, then reduce the heat and simmer, covered, for 30 minutes, or until the apple is mushy. Squash the apple with a potato masher or wooden spoon, if necessary, to break up any lumps.
2 Place a jelly bag in a bowl, cover with boiling water, drain and suspend the bag over a large heatproof bowl.
3 Pour the fruit and liquid into the bag. Do not push the fruit through the bag or the jelly will become cloudy. Cover the top of the bag loosely with a clean tea towel, without touching the fruit mixture. Allow the mixture to drip through the bag overnight, or until there is no liquid dripping through the cloth.
4 Place two small plates in the freezer. Discard the pulp and measure the liquid. Pour the liquid into a large pan. Add 1 cup (250 g/8 oz) sugar for each cup (250 ml/8 fl oz) liquid. Stir over medium heat until all the sugar has

dissolved. Stir in the lemon juice. Bring to the boil and boil, stirring often, for 20–25 minutes. Remove any scum with a skimmer or slotted spoon. Start testing for setting point.
5 Remove from the heat and test for setting point by placing a little jelly on one of the plates. A skin will form on the surface and the jelly will wrinkle when pushed with your finger when

setting point is reached. Add the extra sage and stir gently into the jelly without making too many bubbles.
6 Pour immediately down the sides of clean, warm jars and seal. Turn upside down for 2 minutes, then invert and leave to cool. Label and date. Keep in a cool, dark place for 6–12 months. Refrigerate after opening for up to 6 weeks.

When the apple is very soft, squash with a masher or wooden spoon.

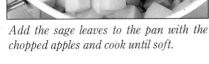

Add the sage leaves to the pan with the chopped apples and cook until soft.

Leave the fruit and liquid to drain through the suspended jelly bag overnight.

TOMATO AND CHILLI RELISH

Preparation time: 20 minutes
Total cooking time: 2 hours 20 minutes
Makes 1 litre (32 fl oz)

1 kg (2 lb) tomatoes
3 cooking apples (500 g/1 lb), peeled, cored and grated
2 onions, chopped
1 teaspoon grated fresh ginger
4 cloves garlic, chopped
1–2 long red chillies, sliced
1 cup (230 g/7¹/2 oz) firmly packed soft brown sugar
1 cup (250 ml/8 fl oz) cider vinegar

1 Cut a cross at the base of each tomato, place in a large bowl, cover with boiling water and leave for 30 seconds, or until the skins start to spilt. Transfer to a bowl of cold water. Peel away the skin, roughly chop the tomatoes and place in a large pan.
2 Add the remaining ingredients to the pan and stir over low heat until all the sugar has dissolved. Bring to the boil, then reduce the heat and simmer, stirring often, for 2–2¹/4 hours, or until the relish has reduced and thickened.
3 Spoon immediately into clean, warm jars, and seal. Turn the jars upside down for 2 minutes, then invert and leave to cool. Label and date. Leave for 1 month before opening to allow the flavours to develop. Store in a cool, dark place for up to 12 months. Refrigerate after opening for up to 6 weeks.

COOK'S FILE

Serving suggestion: Serve with cooked or cold meats, or at a barbecue.

Cut a cross in the base of the tomatoes to make the skin peel away more easily.

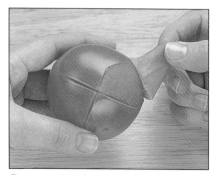

Remove the skin from the tomatoes, starting from the cross.

Allow the mixture to simmer until it has reduced and thickened.

PINEAPPLE CHUTNEY

Preparation time: 30 minutes
Total cooking time: 1 hour 35 minutes
Makes 1 litre (32 fl oz)

1 kg (2 lb) ripe pineapple
2 onions, chopped
1/2 teaspoon ground ginger
1/2 teaspoon ground cloves
1 teaspoon ground cinnamon
3/4 cup (165 g/5 1/2 oz) firmly
    packed soft brown sugar
1/2 cup (125 ml/4 fl oz) white
    wine vinegar
1/2 cup (60 g/2 oz) raisins

1 Peel the pineapple and remove the tough eyes. Cut into quarters, remove and discard the hard centre core and dice the flesh. Combine with the onion, ginger, cloves, cinnamon, sugar, vinegar and raisins in a large pan and stir over low heat until all the sugar has dissolved.
2 Bring the mixture to the boil, then reduce the heat and simmer for 1 1/2 hours, stirring often, until the mixture has reduced and thickened and the pineapple is soft.
3 Spoon immediately into clean, warm jars, and seal. Turn the jars upside down for 2 minutes, then invert and leave to cool. Label and date. Leave for 1 month before opening to allow the flavours to develop. Store in a cool, dark place for up to 12 months. Refrigerate after opening for up to 6 weeks.

COOK'S FILE

Note: The pineapple is ripe if it has a fragrant pineapple aroma and the central leaf pulls out easily.
Serving suggestion: Serve with roast pork or ham, or with deli meats.

Remove the skin and any tough eyes from the pineapple.

Cut the pineapple into quarters and remove the hard core.

Seal the jars, then turn them upside down for 2 minutes.

MUSTARDS

Mustards are very simple to make and taste delicious with roasts or cold meats. To allow the mustard flavours to fully develop, store sealed in a cool place for 1–3 weeks. Ensure that the mustard reaches the top of the jar being used as it can dry out on top during storage. Mustards can keep for up to 3 months unopened, but should be stored in the refrigerator once opened.

WHOLEGRAIN MUSTARD

Combine 40 g (1¼ oz) brown or black mustard seeds with 60 g (2 oz) yellow mustard seeds in a bowl. Add ½ cup (125 ml/4 fl oz) white wine vinegar. Cover and leave overnight. Place two-thirds of the seeds, 2 extra tablespoons white wine vinegar, 1 teaspoon salt and 2 teaspoons lemon juice in a food processor or mortar and pestle. Process until coarsely crushed, then transfer to a bowl and stir in the remaining mustard seeds. Spoon into clean jars, then seal, label and date.
Makes 1 cup (250 g/8 oz)

TARRAGON MUSTARD

Put 100 g (3½ oz) yellow mustard seeds in a bowl and pour in ½ cup (125 ml/4 fl oz) tarragon vinegar. Cover and leave overnight. Put the mustard seeds, 2 extra tablespoons tarragon vinegar, 2 teaspoons lemon juice, 1 teaspoon salt and 2 teaspoons dried tarragon in a food processor or mortar and pestle. Process until the seeds are partially crushed. Spoon into clean jars, then seal, label and date.
Makes 1 cup (250 g/8 oz)

GRAINY SWEET MUSTARD

Combine 30 g (1 oz) brown or black mustard seeds with 70 g (2¼ oz) yellow mustard seeds in a bowl. Add ½ cup (125 ml/4 fl oz) white wine vinegar. Cover and leave overnight. Place three-quarters of the seeds, 1 teaspoon salt, 2 teaspoons lemon juice and 1 tablespoon honey in a food processor or mortar and pestle. Process until roughly crushed, then transfer to a bowl and stir in the remaining mustard seeds. Spoon into clean jars, then seal, label and date.
Makes 1 cup (250 g/8 oz)

HONEY MUSTARD

Combine 8 tablespoons honey, 4 tablespoons yellow mustard powder, 4 tablespoons cider vinegar and 2 tablespoons olive oil in a small pan. Mix well and stir constantly over medium heat for 5 minutes, or until thickened. Spoon into clean jars, then seal, label and date.
Makes ⅔ cup (170 g/5½ oz)

TRADITIONAL ENGLISH MUSTARD

Mix 160 g (5½ oz) yellow mustard powder with ⅔ cup (170 ml/5½ fl oz) water or milk to make a smooth, spreadable paste. Stir in 2 teaspoons salt. Spoon into clean jars, then seal, label and date. Keep refrigerated for up to 1 week.
Makes 1 cup (250 g/8 oz)

GARLIC MUSTARD

Put 100 g (3½ oz) yellow mustard seeds in a bowl and pour in ½ cup (125 ml/4 fl oz) white wine vinegar. Cover and leave overnight. Place half the seeds, 2 extra tablespoons white wine vinegar, 1 teaspoon salt, 2 teaspoons lemon juice and 6 crushed garlic cloves in a food processor. Process until the seeds are coarsely crushed, then transfer to a bowl and stir in the remaining mustard seeds. Spoon into clean jars, then seal, label and date.
Makes 1 cup (250 g/8 oz)

SUN-DRIED TOMATO MUSTARD

Combine 40 g (1¼ oz) brown or black mustard seeds with 60 g (2 oz) yellow mustard seeds in a bowl. Add ½ cup (125 ml/4 fl oz) white wine vinegar. Cover and leave overnight. Put 100 g (3½ oz) drained sun-dried tomatoes in a food processor and process until finely chopped. Add half the mustard seeds, 2 extra tablespoons white wine vinegar, 1 tablespoon lemon juice and 1 teaspoon salt. Process until nearly smooth (you may need to do this in batches). Transfer to a bowl and stir in the remaining mustard seeds. Spoon into clean jars, then seal, label and date.
Makes 1½ cups (375 g/12 oz)

Clockwise from top left: Wholegrain mustard; grainy sweet mustard; tarragon mustard; traditional English mustard; garlic mustard; honey mustard; sun-dried tomato mustard.

CHILLI AND GARLIC SAUCE

Preparation time: 20 minutes +
  15 minutes soaking
Total cooking time: 15 minutes
Makes 1 cup (250 ml/8 fl oz)

8 large dried chillies
4 medium fresh red chillies
4 cloves garlic
1/2 cup (125 ml/4 fl oz) white
  vinegar
3/4 cup (185 g/6 oz) sugar
1 tablespoon fish sauce

1 Remove the stem and seeds from the dried chillies, and break into large pieces. Place in a bowl, cover with boiling water and soak for 15 minutes.
2 Meanwhile, cut the fresh chillies in half and remove the seeds. Wear gloves to protect your hands. Finely chop the garlic. Drain the dried chilli and place in a food processor or blender with the fresh chilli and vinegar and process until smooth.
3 Pour into a pan and bring to the boil, then reduce the heat, stir in the sugar and garlic, and simmer for 10 minutes, stirring often, until slightly thickened. Add the fish sauce.
4 Transfer to a heatproof jug and pour immediately into clean, warm jars and seal. Turn the jars upside down for 2 minutes, then invert and cool. Label and date. Leave for 1 month before opening to allow the flavours to develop. Store in a cool, dark place for up to 12 months. Refrigerate after opening.

COOK'S FILE

Note: The heat in the chilli depends on the chillies used and their size. Usually, the smaller the chilli the hotter it is.

Cover the dried chilli pieces with boiling water and soak for 15 minutes.

Process the dried and fresh chilli and the vinegar in a food processor until smooth.

Using a heatproof jug, pour the sauce into clean, warm jars.

AUTUMN CHUTNEY

Preparation time: 25 minutes
Total cooking time: 1 hour 25 minutes
Makes 1.75 litres (56 fl oz)

500 g (1 lb) firm pears, peeled,
    cored and chopped
500 g (1 lb) green apples,
    peeled, cored and chopped
500 g (1 lb) tomatoes, peeled
    and chopped
500 g (1 lb) onions, chopped

5 celery sticks, sliced
3 cloves garlic, thinly sliced
2 teaspoons grated fresh ginger
350 g (11 oz) sultanas
1 litre (32 fl oz) white vinegar
2 teaspoons ground cinnamon
2 teaspoons ground ginger
2¹/2 cups (460 g/14 oz) lightly
    packed soft brown sugar

1 Combine all the ingredients, except the sugar, in a large pan. Bring to the boil, then reduce the heat and simmer for 45 minutes.

2 Add the sugar and stir until all the sugar has dissolved. Bring to the boil and cook for 30–35 minutes, stirring often, or until the chutney has reduced and thickened.

3 Spoon the chutney immediately into clean, warm jars and seal. Turn upside down for 2 minutes, then invert and leave to cool. Label and date. Leave for 1 month before opening to allow the flavours to fully develop. Store in a cool, dark place for up to 12 months. Refrigerate after opening.

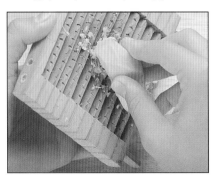

Grate your ginger on a special bamboo grater, or a regular grater.

Combine all the ingredients, except the sugar, in a large pan.

Add the brown sugar to the mixture and stir until dissolved.

ROSEMARY WINE JELLY

Preparation time: 30 minutes +
  overnight draining
Total cooking time: 1 hour 15 minutes
Makes 3 cups (750 ml/24 fl oz)

2 kg (4 lb) green apples
3 cups (750 ml/24 fl oz) dry
  white wine
3 1/2 cups (875 g/11 lb 12 oz)
  sugar, approximately
2 tablespoons roughly chopped
  fresh rosemary leaves
large sprigs of rosemary,
  for each jar

1 Wash the apples well and discard the stalks. Cut into chunks and place in a large pan, skins and seeds included. Add the wine and bring to the boil. Reduce the heat and simmer, covered, for 1 hour. Stir a couple of times during cooking to make sure the apples cook evenly.

2 Place a jelly bag in a bowl, cover with boiling water, drain and suspend the bag over a large heatproof bowl.

3 Ladle the fruit and liquid into the bag. Do not push the fruit through the bag or the jelly will become cloudy. Cover the top of the bag loosely with a clean tea towel, without touching the mixture. Allow the mixture to drip through the bag overnight, or until there is no liquid dripping through the cloth.

4 Place two small plates in the freezer. Discard the pulp, and measure the liquid. For each cup (250 ml/8 fl oz) liquid, allow 1 cup (250 g/8 oz) sugar. Heat the liquid in a large pan and add the sugar. Stir, without boiling, for 5 minutes, or until all the sugar has

dissolved. Remove any scum with a skimmer or slotted spoon.

5 Place the rosemary leaves onto a square piece of muslin and tie securely with string, then add to the pan. Boil for 10 minutes, then remove from the heat and test for setting point.

6 Remove the pan from the heat and test for setting point by placing a little jelly on one of the plates. A skin will form on the surface and the jelly will wrinkle when pushed with your finger when setting point is reached. Discard the muslin bag.

7 Place a sprig of rosemary into each clean, warm jar, and immediately pour the jelly down the sides of the jar and seal. Turn upside down for 2 minutes, then invert and leave to cool. Label and date. Store in a cool, dark place for 6–12 months. Refrigerate after opening for up to 6 weeks.

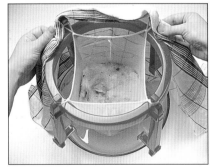

Pour the mixture into a suspended jelly bag and leave to strain through.

Remove any scum from the surface with a skimmer or slotted spoon.

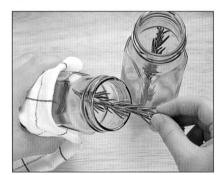

Put a sprig of rosemary into each warm jar before pouring in the jelly.

RED CAPSICUM SAUCE

Preparation time: 30 minutes
Total cooking time: 2 hours
Makes 1.5 litres (48 fl oz)

2 kg (4 lb) red capsicums
2 tomatoes
1 large onion, chopped
1 small green apple, peeled,
    cored and chopped
3/4 cup (165 g/5 1/2 oz) firmly
    packed soft brown sugar
2 cups (500 ml/16 fl oz)
    cider vinegar
2 teaspoons black
    peppercorns
2 tablespoons roughly chopped
    fresh basil leaves

1 teaspoon cloves
1 bay leaf
3 cloves garlic

1 Preheat the oven to moderately hot 200°C (400°F/Gas 6). Roast the capsicums for 35 minutes, or until the skin blisters and blackens. Cut into quarters, remove the skins, seeds and membrane, and chop the flesh.
2 Score a cross in the base of the tomatoes, place in a heatproof bowl and cover with boiling water. Leave for 30 seconds then transfer to cold water and peel the skin away from the cross. Roughly chop the flesh.
3 Put the capsicum, tomato, onion and apple in a food processor or blender and process until finely chopped. Place in a large pan with the

sugar, vinegar and 1 teaspoon salt. Put the peppercorns, basil, cloves, bay leaf and garlic onto a square piece of muslin, tie with string and add to the pan.
4 Stir over low heat until all the sugar has dissolved. Bring to the boil, then reduce the heat and simmer, stirring often, over low–medium heat, for 1 hour 15 minutes, or until the sauce is thick and pulpy. Process in a food processor or blender until smooth.
5 Pour immediately into clean, warm bottles or jars and seal. Turn upside down for 2 minutes, then invert and leave to cool. Label and date. Leave for 1 month before opening to allow the flavours to develop. Store in a cool, dark place for up to 12 months. Refrigerate after opening.

Roast the capsicum and then remove the skin, seeds and membrane.

Score the bottom of each tomato, place in a bowl and cover with boiling water.

Put the peppercorns, basil, cloves, bay leaf and garlic in a muslin bag.

PEACH AND CHILLI CHUTNEY

Preparation time: 20 minutes
Total cooking time: 1 hour 20 minutes
Makes 1.5 litres (48 fl oz)

4–6 medium red chillies
   (about 20 g/³/4 oz)
2 kg (4 lb) ripe slipstone peaches
2 cups (500 ml/16 fl oz)
   white wine vinegar
2 cups (500 g/1 lb) sugar
1 large onion, chopped
1 cup (125 g/4 oz) sultanas

2 tablespoons grated fresh ginger
1 cinnamon stick
rind of 1 orange, cut into strips

1 Cut the chillies in half lengthways, remove the seeds and finely chop the flesh. Wear latex or rubber gloves to protect your hands.
2 Cut a small cross in the base of each peach. Immerse in boiling water for 30 seconds, then drain and cool slightly. Peel off the skins, cut in half and remove the stones. Chop the flesh.
3 Combine all the ingredients in a large pan. Stir, without boiling, until the sugar has dissolved. Bring to the boil, then reduce the heat and simmer, for 1¼ hours, or until the chutney is thick and pulpy. Stir often during cooking to prevent the chutney from sticking or burning on the bottom, particularly towards the end of the cooking time. Remove the cinnamon stick and orange rind.
4 Spoon immediately into clean, warm jars and seal. Turn the jars upside down for 2 minutes, then invert and leave to cool. Label and date. Leave for 1 month before opening to allow the flavours to develop. Store in a cool, dark place for up to 12 months. Refrigerate after opening.

Always wear rubber gloves when handling chillies to protect your hands.

Peel the skin off the peaches, starting at the cross end.

Simmer the chutney, stirring often, until thick and pulpy.

CORIANDER AND LIME JELLY

Preparation time: 30 minutes +
overnight draining
Total cooking time: 1 hour 30 minutes
Makes 1.25 litres (40 fl oz)

1.5 kg (3 lb) green apples
½ cup (125 ml/4 fl oz) white
    wine vinegar
4 strips lime rind
6 coriander stalks, roughly
    chopped
2 teaspoons finely grated
    lime rind
½ cup (125 ml/4 fl oz) lime
    juice
3 cups (750 g/1½ lb) caster
    sugar, warmed (see page 5)
2 tablespoons finely chopped
    fresh coriander leaves
green food colouring (optional)

1 Cut the apples into quarters, including the skin and cores. Place in a large pan with the vinegar, strips of lime rind, coriander stalks and 1.25 litres (40 fl oz) water. Bring to the boil, then reduce the heat and simmer, covered, for 40 minutes, or until the fruit is soft and pulpy.
2 Place a jelly bag in a bowl, cover with boiling water, drain and suspend the bag over a large heatproof bowl.
3 Pour the fruit and liquid into the bag. Do not push the fruit through the bag or the jelly will become cloudy. Cover the top of the bag loosely with a clean tea towel, without touching the fruit mixture. Allow the mixture to drip through the bag overnight, or until there is no liquid dripping through the cloth.
4 Place two small plates in the freezer. Discard the pulp. Add the grated lime

rind and juice to the liquid. Measure and pour the liquid into a large pan. Add 1 cup (250 g/8 oz) sugar for each cup (250 ml/8 fl oz) liquid. Stir over low heat until all the sugar has dissolved. Bring to the boil and boil, stirring often, for 40 minutes. Remove any scum during cooking with a skimmer or slotted spoon. Start testing for setting point.
5 Remove the jelly mixture from the heat and test for setting point by placing a little jelly onto one of the

plates. A skin will form on the surface and the jelly will wrinkle when pushed with your finger when setting point is reached. Stir in the coriander and a few drops of colouring.
6 Immediately pour the jelly down the sides of clean, warm jars and seal. Turn upside down for 2 minutes, then invert and leave to cool. Label and date. Store in a cool, dark place for 6–12 months. Refrigerate after opening for up to 6 weeks. Serve with chicken, salmon, pork, or Chinese roast duck.

Cut strips of rind off a lime, taking care to avoid the bitter white pith.

Place the apple, vinegar, lime rind, coriander stalks and water in a pan.

When the sugar has dissolved, boil the mixture for about 40 minutes.

FRUIT PASTES

Fruit pastes are a perfectly delicious method for preserving an overabundance of fruit. They may take a while to cook, but fruit pastes keep well for up to a year because of their high concentration of sugar. They are delicious with coffee, as part of a cheese board or with cold meats.

QUINCE PASTE

Line a 28 x 18 cm (11 x 7 inch) tin with baking paper. Peel and core 2 kg (4 lb) quinces, reserving the cores. Cut into chunks and place in a large pan. Chop the cores, place on a square of muslin, tie securely with string and add to the pan with 2 cups (500 ml/ 16 fl oz) water and 2 tablespoons lemon juice. Cook, covered, over low heat for 30–40 minutes, or until soft and tender. Cool slightly, then squeeze any juices from the muslin bag and discard. Purée the fruit in a blender or food processor until smooth, then press through a fine sieve. Weigh the purée and return it to the pan. Gradually add an equivalent measure of sugar (1 kg/2 lb fruit purée = 1 kg/ 2 lb sugar). Stir over low heat, without boiling, until all the sugar has dissolved. Cook, stirring with a wooden spoon to prevent sticking and burning, for 45–60 minutes, or until the mixture leaves the side of the pan and it is difficult to push the wooden spoon through. (If the mixture starts to stick to the bottom of the pan, transfer to a heatproof bowl, clean the pan and return to the clean pan to continue cooking.)

To package and store the pastes: Spread into the prepared tin and smooth with a palette knife. Cut into small squares, diamonds or triangles with a hot knife. Place a blanched or slivered almond in the centre of each piece or roll in caster sugar to coat, if desired. Wrap in foil and store in an airtight container in a cool, dry place. Disposable foil tins are ideal for storing fruit pastes. Spread the hot fruit mixture into them and press a piece of greaseproof paper onto the mixture before wrapping.

Note: As the mixture thickens, it will start to splatter. Make sure you use a large, deep-sided pan and wrap a tea towel around your hand while stirring.

APRICOT PASTE

Line a 28 x 18 cm (11 x 7 inch) tin with baking paper. Select 2 kg (4 lb) apricots (you will need some to be a little green to help gel the paste). Remove the stalks, stones and any blemishes. Cut the greenish apricots into quarters and the remainder in half. Place in a large pan with 1 cup (250 ml/8 fl oz) water and 2 tablespoons lemon juice. Bring to the boil, then reduce the heat and simmer, covered, for 15–20 minutes, or until the fruit is soft and tender. Cool slightly. Purée the fruit in a blender or food processor until smooth, then press through a fine sieve. Weigh the purée and return it to the pan. Gradually add an equivalent measure of sugar (1 kg /2 lb fruit purée = 1 kg/ 2 lb sugar). Stir over low heat, without boiling, until all the sugar has dissolved. Cook, stirring with a wooden spoon to prevent sticking and burning, for 45–60 minutes, or until the mixture leaves the side of the pan and it is difficult to push the wooden spoon through. (If the mixture starts to stick to the bottom of the pan, transfer to a heatproof bowl, clean the pan and return to the clean pan to continue cooking.)

PLUM PASTE

Line a 28 x 18 cm (11 x 7 inch) tin with baking paper. Select 1.5 kg (3 lb) plums (you will need some to be a little green to help gel the paste). Remove the stalks, stones and any blemishes, then cut into quarters. Place in a large pan with 1 cup (250 ml/ 8 fl oz) water and 2 tablespoons lemon juice. Bring to the boil, then reduce the heat and simmer, covered, for 20–30 minutes, or until the fruit is soft and tender. Cool slightly. Purée the fruit in a blender or food processor until smooth, then press through a fine sieve. Weigh the purée and return it to the pan. Gradually add an equivalent measure of sugar (1 kg/2 lb fruit purée = 1 kg/2 lb sugar). Stir constantly over low heat, without boiling, until all the sugar has dissolved. Cook, stirring with a wooden spoon to prevent sticking and burning, for 45–60 minutes, or until the mixture leaves the side of the pan and is difficult to push the wooden spoon through. (If the mixture starts to stick to the bottom of the pan, transfer to a heatproof bowl, clean the pan and return to the clean pan to continue cooking.)

PEACH PASTE

Line a 28 x 18 cm (11 x 7 inch) tin with baking paper. Remove the stalks, blemishes and stones from 2 kg (4 lb) peaches (you will need some to be a little green to help gel the paste). Cut each peach into 8 pieces and place in a large pan with 1 cup (250 ml/8 fl oz) water and 3 tablespoons lemon juice. Bring to the boil, then reduce the heat and simmer, covered, for 20–30 minutes, or until the fruit is soft and tender. Cool slightly. Pureé the fruit in a blender or food processor until smooth, then press through a fine sieve. Weigh the purée and return it to the pan. Gradually add an equivalent measure of sugar (1 kg/2 lb fruit purée = 1 kg/2 lb sugar) to the pan. Stir constantly over low heat, without boiling, until all the sugar has dissolved. Cook, stirring with a wooden spoon to prevent sticking and burning, for 45–60 minutes, or until the mixture leaves the side of the pan and it is difficult to push the wooden spoon through. (If the mixture starts to stick to the bottom of the pan, transfer to a heatproof bowl, clean the pan and return to the clean pan to continue cooking.)

Clockwise from top left: Quince paste; peach paste; apricot paste; plum paste.

PICCALILLI

Preparation time: 30 minutes +
  overnight soaking
Total cooking time: 10 minutes
Makes 2 litres (64 fl oz)

400 g (13 oz) cauliflower,
  cut into florets
1 small cucumber, chopped
200 g (6½ oz) green beans, cut
  into 2 cm (¾ inch) lengths
1 onion, chopped
2 carrots, chopped
2 celery sticks, chopped
⅓ cup (100 g/3½ oz) salt
1 cup (250 g/8 oz) sugar
1 tablespoon mustard powder
2 teaspoons ground turmeric
1 teaspoon ground ginger
1 fresh red chilli, seeded
  and finely chopped
1 litre (32 fl oz) white
  vinegar
200 g (6½ oz) frozen broad
  beans, thawed, peeled
½ cup (60 g/2 oz) plain flour

1 Combine the cauliflower, cucumber, beans, onion, carrot, celery and salt in a large bowl. Add enough water to cover the vegetables, and top with a small upturned plate to keep the vegetables submerged. Leave to soak overnight.

2 Drain the vegetables well and rinse under cold running water. Drain the vegetables again. Combine the vegetable mixture with the sugar, mustard, turmeric, ginger, chilli and all but ¾ cup (185 ml/6 fl oz) of the vinegar in a large pan. Bring to the boil, then reduce the heat and simmer for 3 minutes. Stir in the broad beans. Remove any scum from the surface with a skimmer or slotted spoon.

3 Blend the flour with the remaining vinegar and stir it into the vegetable mixture. Stir until the mixture boils and thickens.

4 Spoon immediately into clean, warm jars and seal. Turn the jars upside down for 2 minutes, then invert. Label and date. Leave for 1 month before opening to allow the flavours to develop. Store in a cool, dark place for up to 12 months. Refrigerate after opening for up to 6 weeks.

Thaw the frozen broad beans, then squeeze the beans out of the skins.

Add the vinegar and spices to the drained vegetables.

Put an upturned plate on top of the vegetables to keep them submerged.

Blend the flour with the reserved vinegar and stir into the vegetable mixture.

ROASTED TOMATO RELISH

Preparation time: 20 minutes
Total cooking time: 2 hours 50 minutes
Makes 1 litre (32 fl oz)

2 kg (4 lb) tomatoes, halved
2 onions (310 g/10 oz), chopped
2 small red chillies, seeded
   and chopped
1 teaspoon paprika or
   Hungarian smoked paprika
1 1/3 cups (350 ml/11 fl oz)
   white wine vinegar
1 1/3 cups (340 g/11 oz) sugar

1/4 cup (60 ml/2 fl oz) lemon juice
1 teaspoon grated lemon rind

1 Preheat the oven to slow 150°C (300°F/Gas 2). Line a baking tray with foil and then baking paper. Place the tomato halves cut-side-up on the baking tray and cook for 1 hour. Sprinkle with the onion and cook for another hour.
2 Cool slightly, then remove the tomato skins and roughly chop. Place the tomato, onion, chilli, paprika, vinegar, sugar, lemon juice, lemon rind and 2 teaspoons salt into a large pan and stir until all the sugar has dissolved.
3 Bring to the boil, then reduce the heat and simmer for 45 minutes, or until the relish is thick and pulpy. Stir often to prevent the relish from burning or sticking.
4 Spoon immediately into clean, warm jars and seal. Turn the jars upside down for 2 minutes, then invert and leave to cool. Label and date. Leave for 1 month before opening to allow the flavours to develop. Store in a cool, dark place for up to 12 months. Refrigerate after opening for up to 6 weeks.

COOK'S FILE

Note: If available, Hungarian smoked paprika gives this relish a lovely smoky flavour. It is available at speciality spice shops and delicatessens.

Sprinkle the chopped onion over the baked tomato and bake for another hour.

Cool the baked tomatoes slightly, then remove the skins and roughly chop.

Simmer for 45 minutes, or until the relish is thick and pulpy.

TRADITIONAL CHILLI JAM

Preparation time: 20 minutes +
15 minutes soaking
Total cooking time: 20 minutes
Makes 2 cups (500 ml/16 fl oz)

8 large dried red chillies
2 whole heads of garlic
300 g (10 oz) red Asian or
    French shallots
1 cup (250 ml/8 fl oz) peanut oil
100 g (3½ oz) small dried shrimps
1 teaspoon shrimp paste
120 g (4 oz) palm sugar, grated
3 tablespoons tamarind
    concentrate
2 teaspoons finely grated
    lime rind

1 Remove the stems and seeds from the chillies and break into large pieces. Place in a bowl, cover with hot water and soak for 15 minutes. Divide the garlic into cloves. Peel and thinly slice the garlic and shallots. Drain the chilli and pat dry.
2 Heat half the oil in a wok over a medium–low heat and gently fry the garlic, shallots and chilli, stirring often, until golden brown. Remove and drain on paper towels.
3 Place the shrimp in a spice mill, food processor or mortar and pestle and process or pound until fine. Add the shrimp paste and fried garlic, shallots and chilli, and process to a smooth paste.
4 Reheat the wok and add the remaining oil and the paste mixture. Cook for 5 minutes, stirring, or until it is very aromatic. Stir in the palm sugar, tamarind, lime rind, 1 teaspoon salt and 100 ml (3½ fl oz) water.

Bring to the boil, stirring constantly, for 5–8 minutes, or until thickened. Take care not to burn the bottom of the pan. Spoon immediately into clean, warm jars and seal. Store in a cool, dark place for 6–12 months. Refrigerate after opening for up to 6 weeks.

COOK'S FILE

Note: This jam is thick and paste-like and will firm on cooling. Ingredients such as dried shrimps, shrimp paste, palm sugar and tamarind concentrate are available from Asian food stores.

Remove the stems and seeds from the dried chillies and break into pieces.

Fry the garlic, shallots and chilli until golden brown and drain on paper towels.

Add the palm sugar, tamarind, lime rind, salt and water and boil until thickened.

DRIED APRICOT CHUTNEY

Preparation time: 20 minutes +
  2 hours soaking
Total cooking time: 50 minutes
Makes 1.75 litres (56 fl oz)

500 g (1 lb) dried apricots
1 large onion, chopped
3 cloves garlic, finely chopped
2 tablespoons grated fresh ginger
2 cups (500 ml/16 fl oz) cider
  vinegar
1 cup (230 g/7½ oz) firmly
  packed soft brown sugar
1 cup (125 g/4 oz) sultanas
2 teaspoons mustard seeds,
  crushed (see Note)
2 teaspoons coriander seeds,
  crushed
½ teaspoon ground cumin
⅓ cup (80 ml/2¾ fl oz) orange
  juice
½ teaspoon grated orange rind

1 Put the apricots in a bowl, cover with 2 litres (64 fl oz) water and leave to soak for 2 hours. Drain and put 1 litre (32 fl oz) of the soaking water into a large pan. Make up with fresh water if there is not enough. Chop the apricots. Put the apricots and all the ingredients, except the orange juice and rind, into the pan. Add 1 teaspoon salt.
2 Stir the mixture over low heat for 5 minutes, or until all the sugar has dissolved. Bring to the boil, cover and boil for 45 minutes, or until thick and pulpy. Stir often, especially towards the end of the cooking time so the mixture does not stick and burn. Remove any scum during cooking with a skimmer or slotted spoon.
3 Stir in the orange juice and rind.

Spoon immediately into clean, warm jars. Use a skewer to remove any air bubbles, then seal. Turn upside down for 2 minutes, then invert and leave to cool. Label and date. Leave for 1 month to allow the flavours to develop. Store in a cool, dark place for up to 12 months. Refrigerate after opening for up to 6 weeks.

COOK'S FILE

Note: Crushing the mustard and coriander seeds helps to release their aroma. You can use the back of a large, heavy knife to crush the seeds, or a mortar and pestle, or put them in a thick plastic bag and crush them with a rolling pin.

Crush the mustard and coriander seeds to release their aroma.

When the apricots are plump, drain and reserve the soaking liquid.

Add the orange juice and rind to the chutney just before sealing it in the jars.

SWEET CORN RELISH

Preparation time: 15 minutes
Total cooking time: 1 hour
Makes 1.75 litres (56 fl oz)

1 green capsicum, seeded and
    finely chopped
1 red capsicum, seeded and
    finely chopped
3 x 420 g (14 oz) cans corn
    kernels, drained
1 tablespoon yellow mustard
    seeds, crushed (see Note)
2 teaspoons celery seeds, crushed
1 large onion, finely chopped

2¹/₂ cups (600 ml/20 fl oz) white
    wine or cider vinegar
2 tablespoons mustard powder
1 cup (230 g/7¹/₂ oz) firmly
    packed soft brown sugar
1 teaspoon ground turmeric
2 tablespoons cornflour

1 Place all the ingredients, except the cornflour, in a large pan. Add 1 teaspoon salt and stir over low heat for 5 minutes, or until all the sugar has dissolved. Simmer for 50 minutes, stirring frequently.
2 In a small bowl, combine the cornflour with 2 tablespoons water. Add to the pan and cook, stirring, for 2–3 minutes, or until the mixture boils and thickens.
3 Spoon immediately into clean, warm jars. Use a skewer to remove air bubbles and seal. Turn the jars upside down for 2 minutes, then invert and leave to cool. Label and date. Leave for 1 month before opening to allow the flavours to develop. Store in a cool, dark place for up to 12 months. Refrigerate after opening.

COOK'S FILE

Note: Crush the mustard and celery seeds in a mortar and pestle, or place in a plastic bag and crush with a rolling pin, to release the aroma.

Use a mortar and pestle to crush the mustard and celery seeds.

Place the ingredients in a pan and stir over low heat until the sugar has dissolved.

Remove the seeds and white membrane and finely chop the capsicums.

Sprinkle salt over the eggplant and leave for 20 minutes before rinsing.

Add the paste and spices to the onion and cook for a further 1 minute.

Spoon the pickle into clean, warm jars, then seal and date.

EGGPLANT PICKLE

Preparation time: 20 minutes +
   20 minutes standing
Total cooking time: 30 minutes
Makes 1.25 litres (40 fl oz)

2 eggplant (800 g/1 lb 10 oz),
   cut into 1 cm (¹/2 inch) cubes
4 cloves garlic, chopped
50 g (¹/2 oz) fresh ginger,
   chopped
2 red chillies, chopped
¹/2 cup (125 ml/4 fl oz) oil
1 onion, chopped
1 tablespoon ground cumin
1 teaspoon fennel seeds
1 tablespoon ground coriander
¹/2 teaspoon ground turmeric
1 cup (250 ml/8 fl oz) white
   wine vinegar
²/3 cup (160 g/5¹/2 oz) sugar

1 Put the eggplant in a colander set over a bowl and sprinkle with 1 tablespoon salt. Leave for 20 minutes, then rinse well in cold water and pat dry with paper towels.
2 Chop the garlic, ginger and chilli in a food processor, adding a teaspoon of water if necessary, to make a paste.
3 Heat the oil in a large pan, add the onion and cook for 2 minutes, or until soft. Add the garlic paste and the ground cumin, fennel seeds, ground coriander and turmeric, and cook, stirring, for 1 minute. Add the eggplant and cook for 5–10 minutes, or until the eggplant has softened.
4 Add the white wine vinegar, sugar and 1 teaspoon salt, if necessary, and stir to combine. Cover and simmer gently for 15 minutes, or until soft.
5 Spoon immediately into clean, warm jars. Use a skewer to remove any air bubbles and seal. Turn the jars upside down for 2 minutes, then invert and leave to cool. Label and date. Leave for 1 month to allow the flavours to develop. Store in a cool, dark place for up to 12 months. Refrigerate after opening for up to 6 weeks.

CHILLI JELLY

Preparation time: 30 minutes +
    overnight draining
Total cooking time: 1 hour 20 minutes
Makes 1.25 litres (40 fl oz)

**2 kg (4 lb) green apples
rind of 1 lemon, in wide strips
1 cup (250 ml/8 fl oz) red wine
    vinegar
1.25 kg (2 lb 8 oz) sugar,
    warmed (see page 5)
50 g (1¾ oz) red chillies, chopped
whole red chilli, for each jar**

1 Cut the apples into chunks and place in a large pan with 1 litre (32 fl oz) water. Add the lemon rind and vinegar. Bring to the boil, then reduce the heat and simmer, covered, for 1 hour, or until the apples are soft and pulpy. Stir often during cooking.
2 Place a jelly bag in a bowl, cover with boiling water, drain and suspend the bag over a large heatproof bowl.
3 Ladle the mixture into the bag. Do not push the fruit through the bag or the jelly will become cloudy. Cover the top of the bag with a clean tea towel, without touching the fruit mixture, and allow the mixture to drip through the bag overnight, or until there is no liquid dripping through the cloth.
4 Put two small plates in the freezer. Discard the pulp, measure the liquid and pour it into a large pan. Add 1 cup (250 g/8 oz) sugar for each cup (250 ml/8 fl oz) liquid. Stir over low heat until all the sugar has dissolved.
5 Place the chopped chillies on a square of muslin and tie securely with string. Add to the pan. Bring to the boil and boil rapidly for 15 minutes. Then start testing for setting point.

6 Remove from the heat and place a little jelly on one of the plates. A skin will form on the surface and the jelly will wrinkle when pushed with your finger when setting point is reached. Discard the muslin bag. Remove any scum from the surface.
7 Immediately pour the jelly down the sides of the clean, warm jars, dropping a chilli into each jar. Seal, then turn the jars upside down for 45 minutes. Invert the jars and leave to cool. This suspends the chilli in the jars. Label and date. Store in a cool, dark place for 6–12 months. Refrigerate after opening for up to 6 weeks.

Ladle the mixture into the bag and allow to drip through overnight.

Roughly chop the chillies and place, seeds included, in a muslin bag.

APPLE, DATE AND PECAN CHUTNEY

Preparation time: 20 minutes
Total cooking time: 45 minutes
Makes 1.75 litres (56 fl oz)

2 brown onions, chopped
1.2 kg (2 lb 6¹/2 oz) green apples, peeled, cored and chopped into small chunks
400 g (13 oz) dates, seeded and chopped
125 g (4 oz) pecans, chopped

2 teaspoons cumin seeds
2 teaspoons finely chopped fresh ginger
1¹/4 cups (315 ml/10 fl oz) white vinegar
¹/2 cup (125 g/4 oz) sugar

1 Put the onion and ¹/2 cup (125 ml/ 4 fl oz) water in a large pan. Bring to the boil, then reduce the heat and simmer, covered, for 10–15 minutes, or until the onion is soft. Add the apple, and simmer, covered, for 15–20 minutes, or until the apple has softened. Stir often.
2 Add the dates, pecans, cumin seeds, ginger, vinegar, sugar, ¹/2 teaspoon salt and ¹/4 cup (60 ml/2 fl oz) water. Stir over low heat for 5 minutes, or until all the sugar has dissolved, then simmer for 5 minutes, or until thick.
3 Spoon immediately into clean, warm jars. Use a skewer to remove any air bubbles, then seal. Turn upside down for 2 minutes, then invert and leave to cool. Label and date. Leave for 1 month before opening to allow the flavours to develop. Store in a cool, dark place for up to 12 months. Refrigerate after opening for up to 6 weeks. Serve with roast pork, ham, cold meats and cheese.

Remove the seeds from the dates and roughly chop.

Add the apple to the onion and simmer until it has softened.

Add the remaining ingredients to the apple and onion mixture.

CLASSIC MINT JELLY

Preparation time: 30 minutes +
  overnight draining
Total cooking time: 1 hour 20 minutes
Makes 2 litres (64 fl oz)

1.6 kg (3¼ lb) green apples
1 cup (50 g/1¾ oz) chopped
  fresh mint
1 cup (250 ml/8 fl oz) lemon juice
1 kg (2 lb) sugar, warmed
  (see page 5)
⅓ cup (20 g/¾ oz) chopped
  fresh mint, extra

1 Wash the apples well and cut into chunks. Place in a large pan with the mint, lemon juice and 1.25 litres (40 fl oz) water. Slowly bring to the boil, then reduce the heat and simmer for 50–60 minutes, or until the apple is soft. Stir to help break up any lumps. Transfer to a heatproof jug and cool.
2 Place a jelly bag in a bowl with boiling water, drain and suspend the bag over a large bowl. Pour the fruit and liquid into the bag. Do not push the fruit through the bag or the jelly will become cloudy. Cover the top of the fruit in the bag loosely with a clean tea towel, without touching the fruit mixture, and allow the mixture to drip through the bag overnight or until there is no liquid dripping through the cloth.
3 Put two small plates in the freezer. Discard the pulp, measure the liquid and add to a large pan. Add 1 cup (250 g/8 oz) sugar for every cup (250 ml/8 fl oz) liquid and stir over low heat for 5 minutes, or until all the sugar has dissolved. Bring to the boil and boil for 10–15 minutes, stirring often. Remove any scum during cooking with

a skimmer or slotted spoon.
4 Remove from the heat and test for setting point by placing a little jelly onto one of the plates. A skin will form on the surface and the jelly will wrinkle when pushed with your finger when setting point is reached. Gently stir through the extra mint. Stand for 5 minutes, or until the mint just stays suspended in the jelly.
5 Transfer the jelly to a heatproof jug and pour into clean, warm jars and seal. Turn the jars upside down for

2 minutes, then invert and cool. Label and date. Store in a cool, dark place for 6–12 months. Refrigerate after opening for up to 6 weeks. Mint jelly is traditionally served with roast lamb.

COOK'S FILE

Note: Transferring the jelly into a heatproof jug before pouring it into the jar stops it from splashing down onto the base which causes air bubbles to be suspended throughout the jelly.

Cook the apples in water for up to 1 hour, or until softened.

Pour the apples and liquid into a jelly bag and leave to drip through overnight.

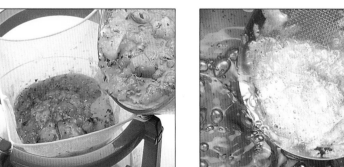

Skim any scum off the surface with a skimmer or slotted spoon.

Peel the skins away from the cooked capsicum and discard.

Add the sugar to the pan and stir over low heat until it has all dissolved.

Remove any scum from the surface with a skimmer or slotted spoon.

RED CAPSICUM JELLY

Preparation time: 20 minutes
Total cooking time: 50 minutes
Makes 1.25 litres (40 fl oz)

5 red capsicums, halved,
    membrane and seeds removed
1 red chilli, seeded and finely
    chopped (optional)
1 cup (250 ml/8 fl oz) white
    wine vinegar
2 tablespoons lemon juice
3 cups (750 g/1½ lb) sugar,
    warmed (see page 5)
50 g (1¾ oz) jam-setting
    mixture

1 Preheat the oven to moderately hot 200°C (400°F/Gas 6). Line a baking tray with foil, place the capsicum on it, cut-side-down, and roast for 40 minutes. If the capsicum starts to blacken around the cut edges, cover loosely with foil.
2 Remove the capsicum from the oven and put in a plastic bag. Leave for 10 minutes to allow the skin to loosen, then peel off and discard. Trim off any burnt edges as you do not want a burnt flavour or colour in the jelly.
3 Place the capsicum in a food processor and blend until smooth. Add the chilli, vinegar, lemon juice and 1 teaspoon salt and blend for another 30 seconds. Place in a large pan with the

sugar and stir over low heat until all the sugar has dissolved. Bring to the boil and add the jam-setting mixture. Continue to boil for 5 minutes, stirring often. Remove any scum from the surface with a skimmer or slotted spoon.
4 Pour immediately into clean, warm jars and seal. Turn the jars upside down for 2 minutes, then invert and leave to cool. Label and date. Store in a cool, dark place for 6–12 months. Refrigerate after opening for up to 6 weeks.

COOK'S FILE

Note: Jam-setting mixture is available in powdered form from most health food shops.

SWEET TOMATO AND EGGPLANT CHUTNEY

Preparation time: 20 minutes
Total cooking time: 1 hour 10 minutes
Makes 1.75 litres (56 fl oz)

2 kg (4 lb) ripe tomatoes
500 g (1 lb) brown onions,
    chopped
500 g (1 lb) slender eggplant,
    finely chopped
4 cloves garlic, finely chopped
2 teaspoons sweet paprika
2 teaspoons brown mustard
    seeds, crushed
2 cups (500 g/1 lb) sugar
2¹/2 cups (600 ml/20 fl oz)
    white vinegar

1 Score a cross in the base of each tomato and place 4–5 at a time in a heatproof bowl and cover with boiling water. Leave for 30 seconds then transfer to cold water and peel the skin away from the cross. Roughly chop and place in a large pan.

2 Add the remaining ingredients to the pan. Add 2 teaspoons salt and stir over low heat for 5 minutes, or until all the sugar has dissolved. Bring to the boil, then reduce the heat and simmer, for 50–60 minutes, or until the chutney is thick and pulpy. Stir often. Remove any scum during cooking with a skimmer or slotted spoon. Do not cook the mixture over high heat or the liquid will evaporate too quickly and the flavours won't have time to develop.

3 Transfer to a heatproof jug and immediately pour into clean, warm jars and seal. Turn the jars upside down for 2 minutes, then invert and leave to cool. Label and date. Leave for 1 month before opening to allow the flavours to

develop. Store in a cool, dark place for up to 12 months. Refrigerate after opening for up to 6 weeks. Serve with cold meats, steak, chicken or fish.

COOK'S FILE

Note: To achieve the richest flavour, it is best to choose very ripe tomatoes for this recipe.

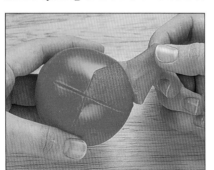

Peel the skin away from the cross scored in the base of the tomato.

Simmer the chutney over low heat until thick and pulpy.

Transfer the chutney to a heatproof jug and then pour into clean, warm jars.

MOSTARDA DI FRUTA

Preparation time: 5 minutes
Total cooking time: 20 minutes
Makes 1 cup (250 ml/8 fl oz)

175 g (6 oz) glacé fruit
1 teaspoon cornflour
1¼ cups (315 ml/10 fl oz)
  white wine
1 tablespoon honey
3 cloves
1 tablespoon yellow mustard
  seeds

¼ teaspoon ground nutmeg
½ teaspoon grated fresh
  ginger
2 cinnamon sticks, broken
  into pieces
1 tablespoon lemon juice

1 Using a pair of scissors, chop the fruit into even-sized pieces. Mix the cornflour with 1 teaspoon water and blend to a paste.
2 Place 200 ml (6½ fl oz) water in a pan with the wine, honey, cloves, mustard seeds, nutmeg, ginger and cinnamon sticks. Bring to the boil, add

the cornflour mixture and simmer for 5 minutes, or until the mixture thickens.
3 Add the glacé fruit and lemon juice, and simmer for 10–15 minutes, or until the fruit is soft and the mixture is thick. Spoon immediately into clean, warm jars and seal. Turn upside down for 2 minutes, then invert and leave to cool. Label and date. Store for a week before eating.

COOK'S FILE

Note: Mostarda di fruta is eaten in Italy with cold meats, poultry and game. It has a very sweet flavour.

Use scissors to chop the glacé fruit into even-sized pieces.

Measure a tablespoon of mustard seeds and add to the pan.

When the mixture has thickened, add the fruit and lemon juice.

SPICY DRIED FRUIT CHUTNEY

Preparation time: 20 minutes
Total cooking time: 1 hour 35 minutes
Makes 2.5 litres (80 fl oz)

400 g (13 oz) dried apricots
200 g (6¹/2 oz) dried peaches
200 g (6¹/2 oz) dried pears
250 g (8 oz) raisins
200 g (6¹/2 oz) pitted dates
250 g (8 oz) onions
250 g (8 oz) green apples,
   peeled and cored
4 cloves garlic, finely chopped
1 teaspoon ground cumin
1 teaspoon ground coriander
1 teaspoon ground cloves
1 teaspoon ground cayenne pepper
3¹/4 cups (600 g/1¹/4 lb) lightly
   packed soft brown sugar
2¹/2 cups (600 ml/20 fl oz) malt
   vinegar

1 Finely chop the apricots, peaches, pears, raisins, dates, onions and apples. Place in a large pan. Add the garlic, cumin, coriander, cloves, cayenne pepper, sugar, vinegar, 2 teaspoons salt and 3 cups (750 ml/ 24 fl oz) water to the pan.

2 Stir over low heat until all the sugar has dissolved. Increase the heat and bring to the boil, then reduce the heat and simmer, stirring often, over medium heat for 1¹/2 hours, or until the mixture has thickened and the fruit is soft and pulpy. Do not cook over high heat because the liquid will evaporate too quickly and the flavours will not have time to fully develop.

3 Spoon immediately into clean, warm jars, and seal. Turn upside down for 2 minutes, then invert and leave to cool. Label and date. Leave for 1 month before opening to allow the flavours to develop. Store in a cool, dark place for up to 12 months. Refrigerate after opening.

Finely chop the dried pears into small, even-sized pieces.

Add all the spices to the fruit mixture before cooking.

Simmer over medium heat until the mixture is soft and pulpy.

INDEX

INTERNATIONAL GLOSSARY OF INGREDIENTS

capsicum	red or green pepper	fresh coriander	fresh cilantro
eggplant	aubergine	tomato purée (Aus.)	sieved crushed tomatoes/
tomato paste (Aus.)	tomato purée, double		passata (UK)
	concentrate (UK)	zucchini	courgette

Published by Murdoch Books®, a division of Murdoch Magazines Pty Limited,
GPO Box 1203, Sydney NSW 1045.

Managing Editor: Rachel Carter **Editors:** Anna Sanders, Jane Price, Justine Upex **Designer:** Michelle Cutler **Food Director:** Jody Vassallo **Food Editors:** Roslyn Anderson, Kathy Knudsen **Recipe Development:** Roslyn Anderson, Amanda Cooper, Gladys Cutler, Michelle Earl, Jo Glynn, Lulu Grimes, Margaret Harris, Malini Jayaganesh, Kathy Knudsen, Michelle Lawton, Barbara Lowery, Kerrie Mullins, Sally Parker, Jo Richardson, Tracy Rutherford, Dimitra Stais, Alison Turner **Home Economists:** Michelle Lawton, Beth Mitchell, Kerrie Mullins, Justine Poole, Margot Smithyman **Photographers:** Jon Bader, Reg Morrison (steps) **Food Stylist:** Jane Hann **Food Preparation:** Justine Poole, Michelle Lawton **Food Technology Liaison Officer, Food Science Australia:** Brigitte Cox **CEO & Publisher:** Anne Wilson **International Sales Director:** Mark Newman.

National Library of Australia Cataloguing-in-Publication Data. Homemade jams and preserves. ISBN 0 86411 708 6. 1. Canning and preserving. 2. Cookery (Jam). 3. Cookery (Relishes). I. Title: Homemade jams and preserves. II. Title: Family circle (Sydney, N.SW). (Series: Family circle step-by-step). 641.852. First printed 1999. Printed by Prestige Litho, Queensland. PRINTED IN AUSTRALIA.